CHINA'S DISRUPTORS

P9-ECW-470

'This is the book for every person who is wondering how China's explosive growth in business is going to impact the rest of the world'
Zhang Ruimin, Chairman of the Board of Directors and CEO, Haier Group

'*China's Disruptors* is a must-read for understanding the next phase of China's economic development. It provides deep insight for all those who do business in China today or who want to participate in this dynamic economy'
Sandra E. Peterson, Group Worldwide Chairman, Johnson & Johnson

'A detailed and fascinating study of the changing landscape in China and the entrepreneurs who are driving that change forward. This is a book that will only become increasingly important in the years to come'
Chen Dongsheng, Chairman and CEO, Taikang Life Insurance Co. Ltd and President, China Entrepreneurs Forum

'Because of Edward Tse's unique access to the people who shape China's economy, this book provides unparalleled insight into the life stories of China's business leaders'
Michael Diekmann, Chairman of the Board of Management, Allianz SE

'No one can explain what is happening in China better than Edward Tse. The rapidly changing China is at yet another important crossroad and you will appreciate his guidance'
Sam Su, Vice Chairman of the Board and Chairman and CEO, China Division of YUM! Brands, Inc.

'For those who think Silicon Valley is the epicentre of technology, Edward Tse will convince you otherwise. *China's Disruptors* is an insightful and thought-provoking look at the "other" game changers. It's a great read for anyone with a passion for innovation and a relentless drive to win'
Dinesh Paliwal, Chairman, President and CEO, Harman International

'In the Internet era, China has outpaced most advanced countries in terms of new technology adaptation and economic growth. In this book, Edward Tse clearly illustrates how China's explosive growth in business will continue to impact the whole country and the rest of the world'
Yu Gang, PhD, Chairman and co-founder, Yihaodian

'Edward Tse is to Chinese corporate strategy what Kenichi Ohmae was to Japanese corporate strategy. This is a book that I could not put down – a deeply insightful book on China that no Chinese strategist or analyst, let alone corporate captain, can ignore'
Andrew Sheng, former Chairman, Hong Kong Securities and Futures Commission and Chief Adviser, China Banking Regulatory Commission

'Edward Tse is an influential thinker in the Chinese business community given his unique background coupled with global knowledge and perspective. *China's Disruptors* will enlighten global business leaders with new visions coming from China'
Wang Wei, Chairman, China Mergers & Acquisitions Association

'*China's Disruptors* provides a bird's-eye view of the entrepreneurs driving growth and innovation in China. Edward Tse's insights into how China's leading businesses will shape the future are important for understanding the global marketplace. These insights along with the personal stories of China's business leaders make for a fascinating read'
Nancy McKinstry, CEO and Chairman of the Executive Board, Wolters Kluwer, NV

'Edward Tse explores very clearly the rise of China's entrepreneurs and the opportunities their rise will generate. After I read the book it became clear to me how global businesses will inevitably have to become more "Chinese" in their manner of operating'
Ronnie Leten, President and CEO, Atlas Copco AB

'This book will change the way you view China, even if you think you are an expert. Edward Tse uses his unique insights and knowledge of China's homegrown entrepreneurs to craft the story of the country's emergence as a global powerhouse driven by innovative disruptors. A must-read'
Rakesh Kapoor, CEO, Reckitt Benckiser Group plc

'In *China's Disruptors*, Edward Tse provides the kind of insight that only comes from a true insider. If you want to understand what's behind the unprecedented growth of China's private sector and what it means for the rest of the world, read this book'
Feng Lun, Chairman of the Board, Vantone Holdings Co. Ltd

'An amazing book on Chinese entrepreneurs who are reshaping the Chinese economy and perhaps the world in the longer term. It helps business people from the West to better understand how this major new force has come about and how it might change the economic landscape worldwide'
Vincent H. S. Lo, GBS, JP; Chairman, Shui On Group

'Essential insights about an emerging class of competitors from China who will dramatically change the competitive playing field as we know it, told by China's leading global strategy consultant, Dr Edward Tse'
Ronald R. Haddock, Vice President, Strategy and Business Transformation, Johnson Controls

'Edward Tse offers a fascinating and insightful journey through the successive generations of spirited entrepreneurs who overcame a once business-averse environment to shape China's free enterprise'
Olivier Bohuon, CEO, Smith & Nephew Plc

'Edward Tse has been discussing the eventual onslaught of China's disruptors for well over a decade. The day when these disruptors are on the world stage and are changing the economics and geopolitics of business is finally upon us. If you're running a global business in any industry, the Chinese disruptors will reshape your business. No one understands that better than Ed and no one can tell the story in such a compelling fashion. A must-read for today's business leaders'
Shane Tedjarati, President and CEO, High Growth Regions, Honeywell

'China will become, if it is not already, the most important market for all high-growth companies in the world. Edward Tse's book will provide important insights to the decision makers in these companies'
Antony Leung, Group CEO, Nan Fung Group; former Financial Secretary, Hong Kong Special Administrative Region Government

'Edward Tse has perfectly captured what today's China's economy is made of. China's disruptors, often looked down upon by their Western counterparts, are the main drivers behind China's dynamism today. We in the West have much to learn from them. Today, China's disruptors; tomorrow, the world's disruptors'
Roland Decorvet, former Chairman and CEO, Nestlé Greater China

'In *China's Disruptors*, Edward Tse takes us into the fascinating world of China's leading entrepreneurs. In the process, he shows us a business community that is far more adaptive, flexible, open-minded and innovative than international observers realize. *China's Disruptors* is a must-read for those who wish to understand the companies and entrepreneurs that are changing China and eventually the world'
Michael J. Enright, Sun Hung Kai Professor, University of Hong Kong and Director, Enright, Scott & Associates

'A useful corrective for those who regard China as a calcified state-driven economy and underestimate the changes taking place'
Financial Times

ABOUT THE AUTHOR

Edward Tse is the founder and CEO of Gao Feng Advisory Company, a global strategy consulting firm with roots in China. As well as helping hundreds of companies – both inside and outside China – develop and apply their strategies, he has also worked with the World Bank, the Asian Development Bank and the Chinese government on issues related to China's economic re-form policies. The author of *The China Strategy*, he has contributed essays and articles to *Harvard Business Review*, *strategy + business*, *South China Morning Post* and *China Daily*. He lives in Hong Kong and Shanghai.

CHINA'S DISRUPTORS

HOW ALIBABA, XIAOMI, TENCENT AND OTHER COMPANIES ARE CHANGING THE RULES OF BUSINESS

EDWARD TSE

PORTFOLIO
PENGUIN

PORTFOLIO PENGUIN

UK | USA | Canada | Ireland | Australia
India | New Zealand | South Africa

Penguin Books is part of the Penguin Random House group of companies
whose addresses can be found at global.penguinrandomhouse.com.

First published in the United States of America by Portfolio/Penguin,
an imprint of Penguin Publishing Group, a division of Penguin Random House LLC 2015
Published in Great Britain by Portfolio Penguin 2015
This edition published 2016
001

Printed in Great Britain by Clays Ltd, St Ives plc

A CIP catalogue record for this book is available from the British Library

ISBN: 978–0–241–24039–7

www.greenpenguin.co.uk

Penguin Random House is committed to a
sustainable future for our business, our readers
and our planet. This book is made from Forest
Stewardship Council® certified paper.

CONTENTS

7

AUTHOR'S NOTE

Over the last two and a bit decades, based in Shanghai, Beijing, and Hong Kong, and working in many other cities across China, I have had the perfect seat to watch the extraordinary transformation of the world's most populous country from economic also-ran to global superpower.

Except, of course, countries don't transform themselves—transformations are wrought by people.

This book is about the people who are largely responsible for that transformation. Not the political leaders, who, important as they were in creating the conditions for business to take off, are not directly responsible for economic growth. Nor China's state-owned enterprises, which—contrary to widespread popular belief—have seen their importance in the Chinese economy decline sharply. But, of course, its entrepreneurs—those people who actually set up businesses and grew them by delivering the goods and services that people were prepared to pay for, and in the process creating the jobs that would allow people to buy those goods and services.

Throughout this book, I refer to the individuals who run those businesses and the companies they have established as being part of China's private sector. But a brief note of clarification is necessary to explain exactly who I'm talking about, as figuring out how much of China's economy is in private hands—or even what a private business is in China—is far from straightforward. Officially, private businesses have only existed in China since 1988, when the government passed legislation allowing them to exist. That legislation defined a private company as a for-profit organization owned by one or more individuals and employing more than eight people. It is a definition that excludes all those businesses owned and run by individuals that have eight or fewer employees. These are sometimes referred to as individually owned businesses and sometimes as sole proprietorships, and China has tens of millions of them. Also excluded from this definition are the many other Chinese firms that are in effect private. The most numerous of these are "red hat" businesses—companies whose underlying ownership lies with individuals, but which for one reason or another (usually to maintain a relationship with local officials) have registered themselves as collective or state-owned businesses. These companies usually pay a "fee," typically a few percent of revenue, in return for protection from official harassment. A variation on the red hat business is the "rented collective"—a collective business that is rented from its original owners, who more often than not are the local government.

A couple of examples show how confused company ownership can be. One of China's most entrepreneurial companies of the last 30 years is white goods maker Haier. Technically, Haier is classified as a collective business under the city of Qingdao, which in theory means that it is owned by its employees and answerable to the Qingdao government. Occasionally, especially in its earlier days, officials would lean on the company to do their bidding; on one occasion Haier took over a money-losing pharmaceutical company in order to keep it running and preserve jobs. While the government may ultimately retain the final say—in the early 2000s, for example, it ruled out the possibility of large collective and state-owned companies being bought out by their managers—Haier's success has left it effectively an independent entity. Over the last 30 years, there can be no doubt that the biggest force determining its destiny has been Zhang Ruimin, its chief executive and board chairman. Ever since he was installed as Haier's head in 1984, it has been his vision and will power that has driven the company forward, not that of its ostensible owners, reflecting just how much, in China, especially in business, power and authority continues to be acquired and held through informal networks rather than legal structures.

Huawei, the Shenzhen-based telecom equipment maker, is another company with somewhat confusing ownership. Company spokespeople repeatedly describe their firm as being an employee-owned private business. As with Haier, however, that description makes little sense: for its entire existence, the company has, for all intents and purposes, been answerable to its founder, Ren Zhengfei, despite his officially holding just 1.4 percent of the company's shares.

Complicating matters further, some entrepreneur-run companies are private but not Chinese-owned. Alibaba, for example, has been majority-owned by foreign companies for many years, thanks to Softbank's 34 percent stake in the company, Yahoo's 22 percent stake (which as of February 2015 was about to be spun off into an independent company), and smaller stakes held by other foreign entities. Moreover, what these businesses own is not a Chinese company itself but stakes in a Cayman Islands company that collects royalties and fees from Alibaba's China-based operations via a string of subsidiaries and "variable-interest entities"—legal structures that in theory offer foreign companies contractual control over Chinese businesses without actually owning them, and so allow them to get around Chinese laws and regulations that bar non-Chinese companies from holding stakes in Internet and other media-related businesses. All of China's other leading Internet companies use similar vehicles. It's a complicated setup, and clearly one with risks: if the government were to change the rules, then such businesses could find themselves operating illegally.

This ambiguity about corporate governance structures, combined with questions concerning the quality of Chinese economic data, make it hard to estimate the size of China's private sector with precision. What we can be sure of, however, is that privately run businesses account for by far the biggest share of the Chinese economy—probably around three-quarters of GDP, and possibly more than 80 percent if we include the country's 100 million or so farming households, each of which is in effect a small business, and its foreign-invested businesses, almost all of which are owned by private companies.

For this book, it's not important whether a business falls into one ownership category or another, but what it is doing and how it is doing it—how businesses such as Huawei, Alibaba, Haier, and Tencent are rewriting the rules in China, changing the country in the process, and creating a market that will, over time, have an enormous impact in the rest of the world.

Quibbling over whether such companies are private or not misses the far more important point—that these are hugely entrepreneurial businesses, run in risk-taking manner, embracing innovation and change, and that running them is a group of extraordinary individuals.

In this book I want to show who these people are, what motivates them, and how they think and act. China's political leaders may have created the conditions under which they operate. But they are the people whose decisions are carrying the country forward. They are creating businesses not just to make money but, as I explore in detail in Chapter 1, as an expression of a far broader and greater mission that includes reestablishing China as one of the world's leading sources of new ideas, technologies, and ways of doing things. Moreover, I believe that these figures have the potential to help not just China but also the world tackle some of the most troubling issues of the 21st century, among them global energy, food security, and climate change.

Things move fast in China. Almost every day brings new developments that could be featured in this book, be they a multibillion-dollar acquisition, a sudden loss in market share, or a new set of government regulations. At the time of this writing, for example, Xiaomi, one of the stars of this book, was having to simultaneously cope with finding itself China's biggest smartphone seller, an attempt by Sweden's Ericsson to halt its sales in India on legal grounds, and government efforts to rein in the power of the United States's Qualcomm, a leading supplier of the technologies used in the components in Xiaomi's handsets. From such a position it could plausibly soar further, taking its China strengths to international markets, or find itself pinned back, losing ground as quickly as it has gained it.

Which trajectory it will follow I have no idea. But what I am confident about is that even if Xiaomi were to crash, another Chinese entrepreneurial company—either one of its existing competitors, such as Lenovo, Huawei, Coolpad, ZTE, Oppo, or a new company that no one has yet heard of—would quickly replace it. In short, I am confident that even if we were to witness the most unlikely reversal in fortune for any of the companies discussed in this book, my fundamental message would remain unchanged: China's future, economically, socially, and—eventually—politically, rests in the hands of its entrepreneurs.

A note on style: throughout this book, I write the names of these people in the standard Chinese way, with the family name first, followed by the person's given name. Yu Gang, for example, is Mr. Yu. If the person has adopted an English name, as with Alibaba's Jack Ma (known as Ma Yun in Chinese) or Tencent's Pony Ma (Ma Huateng), I use standard English usage.

Regardless of whether they have adopted an English name, I am certain of one thing: many more of these figures will over the next few years follow in the footsteps of Jack Ma and Alibaba to become familiar names to Western audiences—because of their astute entrepreneurial skills, and because of the products and services they will bring out of China to the rest of the world.

CHINA'S DISRUPTORS

Company Headquarters

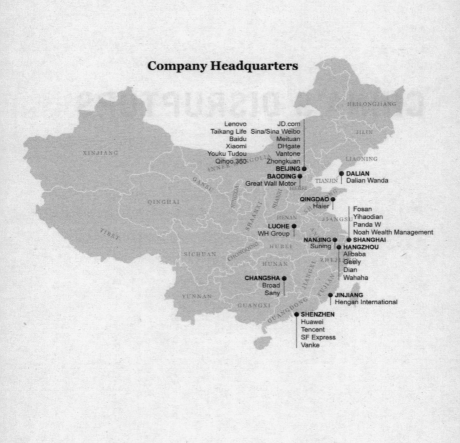

Lenovo
Taikang Life
Baidu
Xiaomi
Youku Tudou
Qihoo 360

JD.com
Sina/Sina Weibo
Meituan
DHgate
Vantone
Zhongkuan

BEIJING ●
BAODING ●
Great Wall Motor

● **DALIAN**
Dalian Wanda

TIANJIN

QINGDAO ●
Haier

Fosan
Yihaodian
Panda W
Noah Wealth Management

LUOHE ●
WH Group

NANJING ● ● **SHANGHAI**
Suning **HANGZHOU**
Alibaba
Geely
Dian
Wahaha

CHANGSHA ●
Broad
Sany

● **JINJIANG**
Hengan International

● **SHENZHEN**
Huawei
Tencent
SF Express
Vanke

ENTERPRISES OF OUR TIME

Zhang Ruimin is a household name in China. Thirty years ago, officials sent him to run a failing maker of poor-quality refrigerators in the coastal city of Qingdao. Today, that company—which he still heads—is better known as Haier, the world's biggest seller of washing machines, air conditioners, and other major appliances. The company's revenues—$29.5 billion—and profits—$1.8 billion—easily exceed those of its two largest global rivals, America's Whirlpool and Europe's Electrolux.

Zhang's achievement in taking an ailing collectively owned factory and building it into a world-beating firm is one of the stunning business success stories of China's reform era. Zhang was born in early 1949, just months before the founding of the People's Republic of China, to parents who worked in a garment factory in north China's Shandong Province. After the disastrous Great Leap Forward economic campaign of 1958 to 1961 and the subsequent famine of the early 1960s, Mao Zedong sought to reclaim his power and prestige by instigating the Cultural Revolution, a nationwide political campaign aimed at purging the Communist Party of his rivals and reestablishing the revolutionary spirit that had brought him to power. Across China, countless young people joined this political movement, launching a long period of chaos and upheaval that left a deep scar on the country.

After the initial fervor of the Cultural Revolution died down, Zhang took his first job, in a construction-materials factory. Through the 1970s and early 1980s, he rose through the ranks to become to a member of the factory's management committee. Along the way, he established a reputation as an autodidact who, despite having ended his formal education at the age of 17, read every business and management book he could lay his hands on. In 1984, Zhang experienced the most pivotal moment of opportunity in his career, though it probably didn't look like one at the time. He was dispatched to run the Qingdao Refrigerator Factory, the fourth director to walk through its doors within the space of a year. When he arrived, he found he was to lead an insolvent, debt-laden plant. "The workshop didn't even have any windows then," he later recalled. "The winter was very cold and the workers had no coal to keep themselves warm, so they removed the window frames and burned them as fuel."

The one thing in the factory's favor was that people wanted what it made. Its refrigerators may have been poorly designed and frequently defective, but China's shortage of consumer goods was so acute that the few people who could afford home appliances would take anything they could get their hands on, regardless of their shortcomings. Of course, this didn't mean customers were happy if their new refrigerators didn't work properly. But for many companies, such matters were of secondary importance. With demand rising fast, especially in the countryside where farmers were taking advantage of reforms that allowed them to sell surplus produce at whatever price they could find, manufacturers of home appliances and other household goods rushed to add capacity, certain they could sell everything they produced.

Zhang, however, was convinced that such circumstances would not continue for long, and that inevitably, as supply rose to meet demand, consumers would become more picky. For a business to thrive in the longer term, he believed, it would need a reputation for reliability and quality.

The following year, in an act that is now legendary in Chinese business history, Zhang addressed this issue head-on. In one of the company's warehouses, he lined up 76 refrigerators that had come off its production line with one problem or another. He asked his staff what they thought they should do with these faulty refrigerators. Sell them at a discount, suggested one person. Offer them to employees, said another. No, said Zhang, we shouldn't be making such refrigerators in the first place. Taking up a sledgehammer—now carefully preserved in a Beijing museum—he destroyed the first of those 76 refrigerators, then forced his staff to follow suit with the other 75.

His statement could not have been more emphatic. From that point on, the Qingdao Refrigerator Factory (shortly afterward renamed Haier) set about establishing a reputation for quality. Zhang instituted rigorous production standards at his factories. To gain access to better technology, he set up a joint venture with Liebherr, a German maker of high-end refrigeration equipment. Inspired by his reading of Japanese management books, he focused on instilling discipline into his workforce. Work processes were improved, and every employee's performance was evaluated on a daily basis. At a time when most companies in China were more interested in simply selling whatever came off their production lines, Haier's focus on establishing itself as the country's first major appliance brand by producing quality products soon started producing results.

In the late 1980s, confident that he could instill similar standards at other factories, Zhang launched Haier on a second stage of development: to acquire the scale that could make it a major player across China. The company expanded its product range to include water heaters, air conditioners, washing machines, and other home appliances. Despite annual profits of less than $10 million, it listed its refrigerator arm on the Shanghai Stock Exchange, raising $400 million. Zhang used this money to build new factories in Qingdao and acquire what he called "stunned fish"—appliance companies that had added capacity to meet China's rising demand but failed to invest in quality control and then found themselves stranded when faced with competition like Haier. In short order, Haier bought eighteen such companies, reviving them by introducing its own quality control measures and adding new products.

Zhang's next move, in the late 1990s, was to take Haier global. As China prepared to enter the World Trade Organization, and more multinationals moved production units to the country, Zhang went the other way, first building factories across Southeast Asia, then investing $40 million to build a refrigerator factory in South Carolina before moving on to open plants in Iran, Italy, Ukraine, Tunisia, Pakistan, Bangladesh, and Nigeria.

Haier added further categories of goods to its portfolio, including televisions, computers, tablets, and mobile phones. The company began to acquire a reputation for innovation, especially for products that met specific local needs: refrigerators with extra-tough cabling that could resist gnawing by rats, and freezers that could stay cool even when their electricity supply was cut off for 100 hours.

Through the 2000s, powered by particularly strong growth in China as the country's urban middle class became homeowners, and by a growing presence in international markets in all parts of the world, Haier overtook its global rivals to become the world's top home-appliance brand by volume in 2009. Assisted by some major international acquisitions, including Sanyo Electric's home appliances arm in 2012 and New Zealand's Fisher & Paykal in 2013, Haier has held on to that position ever since. As of 2014, Haier was the world's fastest-growing company in its sector. In the world of Chinese entrepreneurship, however, no position can be taken for granted. "Who you are or how much you have contributed to the company is not the most important thing," says Zhang. "In this new era . . . there are no successful enterprises—only enterprises of our time."

Since he turned 66 at the start of 2015, it would be understandable if Zhang, having achieved so many milestones already as an entrepreneur, planned to retire. But he has no such intention. Instead, he has now put Haier on course for yet another transformation—one aimed at keeping it relevant to the needs of an economy being turned on its head by the Internet, especially the mobile Internet. "This is a time when everything is changing so fast," he says. "The key factor of traditional sales was location. If you had stores in good locations in a city, that gave you the biggest advantage. During the PC Internet era, the key factor was traffic—whoever had the greatest traffic was the winner. And now in the mobile Internet era, the key factor is time. So my stores are changing from seeking good locations to pursuing the time of customers."

Zhang is one of many entrepreneurs emerging from China who are redefining the nature of business—not just in China, but everywhere in the world. And his relentless urge to keep his company relevant is a quality shared by this entire new wave of Chinese entrepreneurs. This is not a wave driven by the government; it is, if anything, one of the undercurrents of Chinese activity that the government can't quite control—and is not sure how much it wants to control. Haier is among the first Chinese businesses to compete on a world scale, but there are many more to come. The new millionaires and billionaires emerging from China are determined to ride that wave of growth and see how they can shape it to serve their own ends. Indeed, it is the ambitions of China's entrepreneurs to build world-beating companies—private ones—that will be the principal force driving their country's economy to prosper.

A NEW SOURCE OF DISRUPTION

Since the early 1990s, China has consistently been the world's fastest-growing economy. It has opened its economy and its population to the outside world with a speed and success that is unprecedented not just for China but for any country.

In the process, China has also acquired a large number of critics, especially in the United States. These include politicians, among them members of the Obama administration and other key figures in both the Republican and Democratic parties; leading economists such as Nobel prize winner Paul Krugman and Peter Navarro of the University of California, Irvine; and analysts such as Gordon Chang, author of the 2001 book *The Coming Collapse of China*. These critics argue that China's economic success is due, in good part, to unfair practices by the Chinese government: its mercantilist trade regime, its currency manipulation that keeps the value of the yuan artificially low, its high-pressure efforts to open external markets to its businesses, its subsidies for manufacturers, and its widespread pirating of foreign goods and technology. The main beneficiaries of these policies, they say, have been Chinese export manufacturers—those who produce inexpensive smartphones, computers, toys, clothes, and other consumer goods, sucking in jobs from the rest of the world and dumping their products into Europe and America to drive competitors out of business.

Another factor frequently cited by overseas critics is the prevalence and influence of state-owned enterprises in China. The country's biggest companies—its banks and insurers, oil and energy companies, telecom operators and airlines, leading steel, auto, and construction firms—are all government-owned or government-controlled. The Chinese members of the Fortune Global 500, which ranks the world's top companies by revenue, would seem to confirm this view. In mid 2014, some 92 companies on the list were Chinese, but just 10 of these were privately owned enterprises. Using money from China's $4 trillion of foreign exchange reserves, many of these businesses have been investing heavily overseas—been "buying the world," as various book titles and headlines have suggested. Since the early 2000s,

Chinese state-owned firms, backed by state-owned banks, have been striking multibillion-dollar deals in Africa, South America, and other regions, gaining access to energy supplies, raw materials, and even land for farming. Wherever these companies have gone, Chinese construction firms, also state-owned, have accompanied them, building ports, roads, and other infrastructure both to make sure that goods can be shipped back to China and to support the development of their host nations.

But this view of the Chinese economy as a mercantile juggernaut, driven by a single-minded government, does not tell the most dramatic part of the Chinese story, the part with the greatest potential impact on the rest of the world. That is the emergence of a new group of entrepreneurial business leaders, all from the private sector, most of them operating with little direct government influence or support, and all of them transforming their industries. These entrepreneurial disruptors are among the most successful and powerful individuals in China today. Many are billionaires, and some are multibillionaires. They are the reason that (as of August 2014) China hosts the world's second-largest concentration of billionaires after the United States—152 out of the total 1,645, according to *Forbes* magazine.

Haier's Zhang Ruimin is just one of these powerful, creative, and influential entrepreneurs who has changed the face of Chinese business. We will meet many others in this book, among them:

★ **Jack Ma**, whose online empire, the Alibaba Group, towers over China's e-commerce and electronic payments market. Its $25 billion initial public offering in 2014 was the world's largest to date

* **Pony Ma**, whose Shenzhen-based company, Tencent, dominates online games and messaging in China, and is becoming a major rival to Alibaba in e-commerce

* **Robin Li**, the founder of China's leading search engine and social network company, Baidu, which provides more than 60 percent of Chinese search engine activity (Baidu's influence, along with that of Alibaba and Tencent, is such that many commentators refer to this trio of China's three most prominent Internet companies as the BATs)

* **Ren Zhengfei**, the founder of Huawei, China's largest privately owned exporter and the world's leading manufacturer of mobile and fixed-line telecom-network equipment

* **Yang Yuanqing**, who, as chief executive of Lenovo, has built the company into the world's number-one seller of personal computers and a top five seller of smartphones

* **Lei Jun**, a serial entrepreneur whose latest business, Xiaomi, has turned China's smartphone market on its head and become a global rival to Samsung. He uses innovative crowdsourcing techniques to determine the direction of development of his products and sell them with almost no outlay for marketing

* **Yu Gang**, a former Dell executive whose Yihaodian online supermarket, with annual revenues that have risen to nearly $2 billion in just five years, is transforming how urban Chinese buy their daily necessities

* **Li Shufu**, the founder of Geely Auto, China's most successful privately owned carmaker, and one of the most prominent global automakers, thanks to his takeover of Volvo in 2011

* **Xu Lianjie**, a former farmer who has fended off competition from Procter & Gamble, Kimberly-Clark and other Western consumer-goods firms to build Hengan International, China's leading maker of tissues, diapers, and sanitary napkins

* **Diane Wang**, who, after working for Microsoft and Cisco, served as CEO of Joyo.com, an online bookstore launched by Xiaomi's Lei Jun, and then—when that business was sold to Amazon—launched her own global business-to-business Web site, DHgate.com

* **Chen Haibin**, the owner of a chain of medical laboratories pioneering private company involvement in improving standards and choice in China's largely publicly run health-care system

* **Wang Jingbo**, who, since founding Noah Wealth Management in 2005, has signed up more than 50,000 of China's richest people to establish the country's leading private wealth management company

* **Zhang Yue**, a maverick from central China's Hunan Province who, having created a globally successful coolant-free air-conditioning business, now wants to build environmentally sustainable cities using prefabricated modules; to demonstrate the viability of his products and ideas, he is currently

seeking permission to erect the world's highest building in Changsha, Hunan's capital

Not all Chinese entrepreneurs are successful, of course. Like most owners, they have had to take risks with their businesses and their livelihoods. Some failed; many of those started new businesses, learning from their past mistakes. A few fell into legal problems, not because of political rivalries (as you might expect in a country like Russia), but because of their own missteps.

A decade ago, for example, among the most talked-about private Chinese companies was D'Long. A conglomerate based in China's far west Xinjiang region, its annual turnover rose to $4 billion drawn from interests ranging from farming and food to machinery and cement making. Its founder, Tan Wanxin, was for a while the richest person in China before he was sent to jail for manipulating share prices. More recently, in 2010, Huang Guangyu, the founder of Gome Electrical Appliances, one of China's leading electronics retailers who also was China's richest person for a while, was sentenced to 14 years in prison for insider trading and bribery. While D'Long vanished into obscurity following Tan's imprisonment, Gome, despite ups and downs, has maintained its position as one of China's leading retailers in the five years since Huang's jailing.

Most of China's entrepreneurs have fared better than these exceptions. Even if they endured early failures, they have shown phenomenal drive and ability in negotiating the extraordinary changes China and its economy have undergone. The rise of these disruptive entrepreneurs is all the more noteworthy because, at the time of Mao Zedong's death in 1976, China had no private businesses. All of the country's industry and agriculture was publicly owned, run either by the central government, by local governments, or through collectives. Today, thanks to the economic reforms of the last 35 years, the private sector accounts for at least three-quarters of China's economic output.

The Chinese government, despite having long since abandoned central planning, continues to regard itself as playing a key role in managing the overall direction of the Chinese economy. China remains home to approximately 2.3 million state-owned companies. That number, however, is dwarfed by its other businesses. As early as 2004, China had about 3.3 million privately held companies—many owned by investors with shares traded on public exchanges—and 24 million proprietorships—individually or family-run operations. By 2013, the country had nearly 12 million private companies and more than 42 million proprietorships (see Figure 1). Moreover, the government is firmly committed to increasing these totals. In the first seven months of 2014, thanks to regulatory reforms abolishing registered capital requirements, 1.5 million new private companies were set up—double the number during the same period the year before.

The number of state-owned companies, meanwhile, has fallen by almost half since 2004. And though these companies are far more productive than they were a decade ago, their increase in output is a fraction of that of the private sector. In 2000, total revenues earned by state-owned and non-state-owned industrial companies were roughly the same, at about 4 trillion yuan each. By 2013, while total revenues at state-owned companies had risen just over sixfold, those in the non-state sector had risen more than 18 times (see Figure 2). Profits jumped even more over the same period, up nearly seven times for state-owned companies, but up nearly 23-fold for non-state ones.

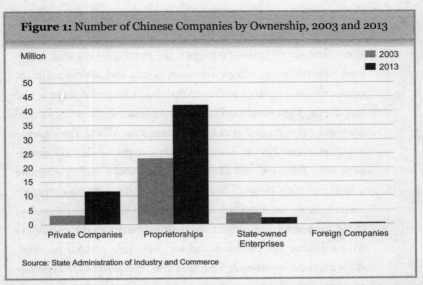

Figure 1: Number of Chinese Companies by Ownership, 2003 and 2013

Million

Legend: 2003, 2013

Private Companies, Proprietorships, State-owned Enterprises, Foreign Companies

Source: State Administration of Industry and Commerce

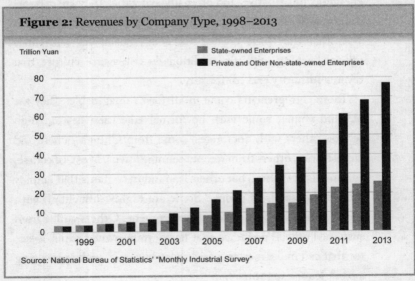

Figure 2: Revenues by Company Type, 1998–2013

Trillion Yuan

Legend: State-owned Enterprises, Private and Other Non-state-owned Enterprises

1999, 2001, 2003, 2005, 2007, 2009, 2011, 2013

Source: National Bureau of Statistics' "Monthly Industrial Survey"

The Chinese entrepreneurs have thrived, in part, because they created companies able to change as China changed. Many of them first set up businesses when the economy was still dominated by the state, which set most prices and appointed most company leaders. They survived the Asian financial crisis of the late 1990s. They fought off competition from the flood of foreign companies that arrived after China entered the World Trade Organization in the 2000s. And they rode out the worldwide downturn that followed the global financial crisis during the late 2000s and early 2010s. Throughout all of this, China's entrepreneurs created an economy largely outside the direct control of the government. They are answerable primarily to the customers who consume the products and services their companies offer. As with their counterparts around the world, they are typically energetic, imaginative, and often idiosyncratic. They are extraordinary individuals in their own right, especially when you consider that they have created successful businesses with little official backing within a traditionally risk-averse culture that reveres authority and conformity.

These entrepreneurs come in all forms imaginable. They are old and young; some with no formal education beyond high school, others with doctorates; some from China's richest and largest cities, others from remote country towns. Most, of course, run small companies, but others lead industry giants that employ tens of thousands of people. Some are highly influential, with access to the highest ranks of government. Others suffer from sustained official prejudice that favors state-owned firms, a factor that can make matters of everyday business, such as securing a bank loan, a nightmare.

Many of today's most successful Chinese entrepreneurs, most

of them now in their 40s, 50s, and 60s, had no experience in business when they started their companies. They had to learn things as they went along through a continual process of trial and error. They were "crossing the river by feeling the stones," as Deng Xiaoping, China's paramount leader from 1978 to 1998, characterized his approach to economic reform.

Among those who started businesses in the period from the 1980s through the early 2000s, not one could have foreseen the China of 2014. Yet these are the people who have played the single biggest role in creating the wealth that exists in China today. Nicholas Lardy, a senior fellow at Washington, D.C.–based Peterson Institute for International Economics and one of the world's leading academic experts on the Chinese economy, estimates that privately controlled companies now account for two-thirds of all urban employment—meaning that almost all of the growth in urban employment since 1978 can be attributed to the private sector.

Chinese entrepreneurs are sometimes compared to the Russian oligarchs of the early 2000s. But the oligarchs built their fortunes by taking advantage of the privatization of industry that followed the collapse of the Soviet Union, often using their connections and positions to amass huge holdings in resource companies. The Chinese entrepreneurs we're looking at in this book, in contrast, have almost all developed their businesses from the ground up, in many instances starting from an apartment or a market stall, or raising a few thousand dollars from friends and relatives. They built their companies by meeting the needs of their customers, often in businesses that no one else saw as feasible.

These business leaders know that they are riding and contributing to a historic wave of economic activity. As creators of the fastest-growing enterprises in the fastest-growing economy in the world, they recognize that they have immense potential influence. Running companies that have grown even faster than the Chinese economy, they are establishing the rules that all companies in China will have to follow. Despite having had almost no formal business training, they are moving rapidly to compete with the same companies from whom they were drawing inspiration just a few years ago, both in China and internationally. In the process, they will rewrite the rules of global management.

SCALE, CHANGE, AND COMPLEXITY

To understand the achievements of these entrepreneurs, we need look no further than China's business environment. China is the only country with the economic scale and robust activity to match that of the United States. Unlike the United States, however, China is still at a relatively early stage of economic development. Its markets have progressively opened wider, and much basic infrastructure has been put in place, but its business environment is still raw and volatile, with a rate of change and pace of activity that is rivaled possibly only by Silicon Valley.

Because of the size of its market, China is the only country likely to produce a rival to Google, Facebook, or Twitter just by building on business established in its home country. Tencent's WeChat, a social networking tool similar at its core to U.S.-based messaging service WhatsApp, had nearly 440 million users in mid 2014 (up from 240 million a year earlier), not far behind WhatsApp's 500 million. Alibaba, likewise, thanks to the nearly $250 billion of business conducted through its various Web sites in 2013 (a figure forecast to rise to around $350 billion in 2014), looks set to become the world's first non-American e-commerce giant.

China will also shape worldwide trends with physical as well as virtual goods. In 2010, it overtook the United States to become the world's biggest manufacturer. As products made in China become more sophisticated and companies embrace more domestically developed technology, it will increasingly be Chinese goods and Chinese consumers that set global standards and preferences. If, as is likely in the near future, Chinese entrepreneurs create a $50 smartphone, or cost-effective solar energy, or mass-produced electric cars, then these offerings will rapidly appear around the world.

On top of its scale and rate of change, China is also hugely complex. Its entrepreneurs have to cope with a country whose markets are not just large and fast-growing, but also at very different stages of development both in different regions of China and often within the same region. Given the speed with which Chinese buying power is rising, products, technologies, and business models often leapfrog entire stages of development. In poorer regions, for example, people can find themselves going from shopping in markets and small family-owned stores to using smartphones to shop online with no intermediate stage. Chinese consumers, presented with a bewildering range of products from domestic, Asian, and multinational brands, are also perhaps the world's most fickle customers. Studies of consumer behavior have repeatedly found that most Chinese show little brand loyalty, whether shopping for everyday goods or big-ticket items. A 2014 survey of 2,400 drivers carried out by the Boston Consulting Group, for example, found that three-quarters planned to switch brands when buying their next car.

And yet, unique as China is in both the size and complexity of its market, I also believe that it is in many ways a harbinger of how the world's business environment will evolve. The main reason for this is technology, especially the ways in which the Internet is bringing down barriers between industries and increasing cross-sector competition. To survive, businesses must look to find new sources of advantage wherever they can, even if this means moving beyond their traditional areas of expertise. Because of the relatively undeveloped nature of its economy, the competitive landscape in China is more fluid than it is in Europe, North America, or Japan. Retailing, for example, is being turned on its head as e-commerce allows shoppers, even in China's most remote regions, to gain access to goods long before stores can build out chains of brick-and-mortar outlets. The country's e-commerce giants are moving into finance, offering money-market products that offer higher interest rates than banks can. Chinese companies are constantly stretching from their established territories into new areas. Computer giant Lenovo and telecom-equipment maker Huawei are both striving to become global smartphone players. Broad Group, a maker of industrial and commercial air-conditioning equipment, now also makes buildings using prefabricated units. BYD, which established itself as a maker of batteries for mobile phones, has now emerged as a viable automaker.

When companies struggle to hold on to any form of competitive advantage, sources of long-term profit become harder to find and retain. As Zhang Ruimin likes to point out, companies can no longer think about establishing a defensible position for themselves and their products; instead, they can only think of creating the means to transform themselves over and over again.

Through the 1990s and 2000s, a lot of Chinese companies set themselves the goal of catching up with multinationals, often benchmarking themselves against what they saw as Western "best practices." Today, having closed the gap, many have realized that they will need to figure out their own paths forward. This is leading to much experimentation, in particular in the area of business strategy, where China's complex, fast-changing, and often ambiguous business environment is making companies rethink how they plan for the future. Rather than setting goals or targets, companies are instead concentrating on ways of strengthening their capabilities to improvise and innovate in the face of immediate challenges and opportunities.

To be successful, entrepreneurs have to seize on the advantages of China's scale and dynamism to make their companies fast-growing, powerful, and flexible, and build around the idea of reinventing themselves repeatedly. Almost all of the Chinese entrepreneurs we'll meet have an extraordinary openness to outside ideas and an increasing willingness to bring in resources from outside China, especially in the form of people with the right kinds of expertise.

REWORKING PERCEPTIONS OF CHINA

The rise of powerful Chinese entrepreneurs will unsettle many people. Early in 2014, China's largest pork producer, WH

Group, a privately owned meat-processing company from Henan Province, reached agreement to buy Virginia-based Smithfield Foods, the United States's largest pork processor, for $7.1 billion. As the deal was completed, Smithfield's CEO, Larry Pope, said he was shocked at the angry reactions he had received from some of his friends and other Americans. Even his mother, he said, had asked him how he could be "selling to the communists."

Outside China, especially in America, such views remain common. The main reason for this is the continued preference of the Western media to depict China's increasing economic and political power as a strategic threat. Many commentators fear that, after taking millions of manufacturing jobs away from North America and Europe, China could now do the same in other sectors, especially if it uses its huge foreign currency reserves to start buying up more and more businesses around the world.

While I don't want to play down the disruption China's reemergence as an international force will cause, this perspective represents a very incomplete perception of Chinese competition. Understanding correctly the nature of the changes in China will be crucial for businesses from around the world both to help them devise their own strategies in response and to figure out what kinds of opportunities will arise that they can take advantage of. Over the next several years, China's entrepreneurial companies will become far more active internationally, entering new markets, acquiring companies, and hiring executives. They will pose enormous threats to established businesses in many industries. Furthermore, for the foreseeable future China's government will almost certainly remain a one-party authoritarian regime with negligible political opposition to continued Communist Party rule.

But to view China as a rival through a Cold War lens is to miss the extraordinary range of forces at play in the country and the direction it will take as its economy develops and its society evolves. While China's governance may be authoritarian, it is also a place of huge, rich, and growing variety. Economically, culturally, and socially, the state has retreated, allowing the country's 1.3 billion people to shape and direct their lives in ways that would have been inconceivable even well into the 1990s. The country's politics are evolving too. Though simplistic notions that the emergence of a middle class would give rise to irresistible pressure for political reform have so far proved unfounded, change has and will continue to occur, shaped by pragmatism both on the part of the country's leaders, who are increasingly sensitive to public opinion, and its citizens, the primary beneficiaries of the last 35 years of economic reforms.

As for China as a global power, other countries are having to adjust to the fact that the global economy has acquired a major new player. The country barely registered on the geopolitical stage a few decades ago, but now it is starting to play an international role commensurate with its scale. Accepting this may be difficult for those countries in Europe and North America that have dominated global decision-making since the Second World War. Throughout history, however, national spheres of influence have risen and fallen. China is now among the world's foremost nations, and no matter what happens next, its reemergence as one of the world's leading economies will affect both economics and politics around the world.

Although I expect China to pursue its interests vigorously, I do not see it seeking to rival or eclipse the United States as the world's hegemonic power. Instead, I see a world which, thanks to the ever-growing interconnections between countries, companies, and people, will require far more accommodation of multiple interests, including China's.

It is important to bear in mind that the new Chinese entrepreneurs do not have preplanned answers to many of the problems that confront them. Their strengths are those of skillful adaptation, in both strategy (what they do) and execution (how they do it). They firmly believe that success will come from pushing onward, takings risks, and reacting quickly to opportunities; from constantly searching for small advantages that will allow them to steal a brief march on their immediate competitors, and larger ones that will enable them to enter a new business area; from building a scale that will make it hard for others to rival their cost base; and from finding new markets, be they emerging new centers of consumption within China or overseas. These entrepreneurs have more options and opportunities than they can follow. They need to choose which industries to enter, what acquisitions to make, and what technologies to develop. Some are focusing their efforts on China while others head overseas in search of untapped markets. For those who seek success abroad, it's not clear which of their China-developed skills will be relevant and which will need to be augmented with know-how from other sources.

A consequence of this is that, while many of the leaders of these companies have a feel for the power they are able to wield, they remain uncertain about how they can best act. They know they must continue to search for new ways of doing things, new variations on their existing goods and services, and new opportunities. But they also know that as they expand and evolve they will be increasingly disruptive—both within China and overseas.

For companies from other countries, the challenge is how to cope with the disruptive forces that the rise of entrepreneurial Chinese businesses will release. This challenge will not only be negative. China, as it becomes more economically competitive and prosperous, will generate an extraordinary range of new opportunities. Part of this will simply be its markets becoming ever more attractive. But China will also grow as a rich source of innovation and knowledge. And it will be a country that is progressively more involved in finding solutions to global problems such as climate change, new sources of energy, and ensuring secure supplies of food and water.

As a business leader working in China, I have been deeply influenced by the achievements of the Chinese entrepreneurs. Over the last 20 years, first as the partner-in-charge of China operations for the Boston Consulting Group when it became the first international strategic consulting firm to open an officially authorized office in China, then as the chairman for Greater China of Booz & Company, and now with my own firm, Gao Feng Advisory Company, I have met all of the major figures profiled in this book. Some I have worked with closely, helping them develop and apply their strategies. Others I have gotten to know at business forums and conferences.

These entrepreneurs are the front line in China's intense hunger for success. I have personally seen how they have taken advantage of their knowledge of Chinese markets to build their businesses, fending off competition from international and other Chinese firms, negotiating with officials over rules and resources, and harnessing the passion and ambition of their employees.

From my many conversations with them, I know that almost all of them combine being intensely Chinese with a truly international outlook. They want to show the rest of the world that their companies can be at least as good as those from anywhere else, but they also know that to realize this goal they will have to draw on best global practices and hire the best people, regardless of where they are from.

I have also seen how their methods and achievements are all too often misinterpreted outside China: attributed to protectionism, copying of products, an undervalued currency, or other unfair advantages. As I hope I make clear in this book, what actually makes these companies so powerful is their relentless focus on developing and delivering products and services that meet the needs and pockets of Chinese consumers and, in more and more cases, those of other countries.

I have written this book to tell their story: their history, their personalities, their business success, and their impact. They have played a remarkable role in China's economic transformation, driving it from a state-controlled to a largely market-driven economy in a mere 35 years. These disruptors will have an even more remarkable impact on the global economy in the future, through the rest of this decade and beyond.

A GUIDE TO CHINA'S DISRUPTORS

This book explores the rise of China's entrepreneurs, the nature of their success and the challenges they pose to existing international companies, and the opportunities their rise will generate.

It explores these themes in the following order.

First, in Chapter 1, I look at what drives China's entrepreneurs to push beyond the normal boundaries expected of even the most successful businesspeople. This chapter examines the features that characterize their approach to business by looking at the various waves of entrepreneurship in China since Deng Xiaoping launched his program of economic reform at the end of the 1970s. An understanding of recent Chinese history is necessary to grasp how a socialist, centrally planned economy became home to the world's most powerful private sector in just three decades, and I provide a primer here.

In Chapter 2, I explore the environment that is producing and shaping these entrepreneurs. I consider China's scale, its market openness, the role of the government, and the role of technology, particularly the Internet, and how these four factors have produced tremendously fast-growing, aggressive, and adaptive companies.

Chapter 3 turns to examine in detail how these companies operate in this environment, and what differentiates them from other businesses around the world, focusing on the way in which they have to constantly find innovative ways to solve the multiple challenges they face. I also argue that, with large-scale government investment in education, science, engineering, and research, China has already laid the foundations for becoming one of world's innovation powers within the next two decades.

Chapter 4 looks beyond China to examine the impact Chinese entrepreneurs have had and will have around the world. To date, Chinese overseas investment has been dominated by large state-owned firms looking to secure the energy supplies and other resources China needs to keep its economy growing. But in recent years, private entrepreneurial companies have been increasing their share of outbound investment. That share will continue to rise, and, far sooner than most people are aware, outbound investment from China will exceed foreign investment into China. As this happens, Chinese entrepreneurs will lead China to become a global economic superpower, opening markets and building and acquiring businesses around the world.

Chapter 5 returns to China to consider the changes the country is undergoing—and the role its entrepreneurs are playing in shaping these changes. It explores how urbanization is creating a country with a very different social, economic, and cultural structure from that which existed just a couple of decades ago. In this chapter, I also describe the institutional changes that will be needed for the country to function efficiently and effectively.

Chapter 6 asks how international companies can react and adapt to the rise of China's entrepreneurs and their companies. Both in China and around the world, businesses will inevitably have to become more "Chinese" in their manner of operating. Partly this will call for integrating their China operations into their global operations—indeed, making them a core part of their global operations—and partly this will require a reworking of their organizational and conceptual frameworks to integrate management practices now taking shape in China.

Finally, in this book's conclusion, I look at the wider implications of Chinese entrepreneurship, beyond business, in the realms of political and social disruption. Ever since Deng Xiaoping launched his country's economic-reform program in the late 1970s, and even more so after he relaunched them in 1992, the entire country has been moving forward on a tide of innovation and risk taking. As a result, I believe that China has embarked on a renaissance that could not just rival its greatest era in history—the Tang dynasty of the seventh through the tenth centuries—but could go a step further and lead to it playing a crucial role in shaping global governance. Thanks to its economic and demographic scale, and, above all, the ambition of its people, China has to become one of the leaders in addressing the key challenges the world faces in the 21st century: coping with climate change and the related issues of food, energy, and resource security. Its demands in these areas have the potential to result in a rewriting of the global norms that have prevailed through the centuries of Western dominance of world politics, with the outcome being a move toward a far greater sharing of international responsibilities.

In China, China's entrepreneurs will play the key role in forming the dynamic economy necessary to create a robust society whose citizens and government will contribute to shaping global development through the coming decades. To understand why I believe this is so, let us turn to those entrepreneurs and consider the animating force which drives them: their spirit.

1

ANYTHING IS POSSIBLE

Is anything impossible for Alibaba's Jack Ma? In September 2014, he floated Alibaba on the New York Stock Exchange, raising more money—$25 billion—than any previous IPO worldwide, making Alibaba the world's fourth-biggest technology company by market capitalization, and confirming Ma's position as China's richest person, with a net worth of $27 billion.

Alibaba dominates online shopping in China. Sales conducted through its various Web sites account for around 80 percent of the country's total e-commerce business, and are worth more than those of eBay and Amazon combined. Its revenues—$7.5 billion in 2013—are comparable with those of Facebook; its profits—$2.85 billion that year—were nearly double Facebook's. In 2014, on November 11, known as Singles' Day, China's biggest shopping day of the year, Alibaba conducted $9.3 billion worth of transactions through its sites, three times more than the online sales transacted three weeks later on Cyber Monday (the first Monday after Thanksgiving) in the United States.

Of course, multiple factors have driven Alibaba's rise, including China's spectacular economic growth and the opportunities that growth has created for businesses. But there's something about Jack Ma that makes you believe he would have succeeded in almost any milieu. One key event stands out in my mind as underpinning Alibaba's entire trajectory—notable not just as a turning point in the company's development, but even more so for it what reveals about Jack Ma's way of driving his company.

In 2004, Ma's original business, Alibaba.com, a business-to-business Web site that linked small and medium-sized Chinese manufacturers with potential buyers around the world, moved into the black, only five years after its launch. Unfortunately, the imminent arrival of eBay in China threatened to siphon off enough of Alibaba's users to end this just-won profitability.

Ma decided to fight, declaring, "eBay may be a shark in the ocean, but I am a crocodile in the Yangtze river. If we fight in the ocean we lose, but if we fight in the river we win." To combat eBay, Ma and his team launched Taobao ("Digging for treasure"), a consumer-to-consumer (C2C) Web site modeled on eBay but with one big difference: unlike its American rival, which charged a transaction fee on all sales, it would offer its services free to both buyers and sellers.

That move was comparatively easy. A far bigger obstacle holding back Taobao's advance—or that of any C2C business in China—was the country's complete lack of an online payments system. Given that credit cards were then held by just 1 percent of the population, consumer e-commerce simply didn't exist.

Ma then had what was probably the single greatest inspiration of his career. If China didn't have a payments system, why not create one? Immediately, he put his staff to work. Across China, Taobao opened bank accounts in branches of every bank in every city, depositing just enough money into each one of them to ensure that transactions would be cleared. Behind the scenes at Alibaba, programmers built systems to record and track the necessary transactions. To make a purchase, a buyer transferred money into one of Taobao's accounts. On receipt of the funds, Taobao notified the seller, who would then dispatch their goods. Taobao only released the funds to the seller once the buyer confirmed the delivery had been received.

Within just a few weeks of Ma's revelation, China had its first secure online payments system in place. It almost immediately began to change the Chinese culture. By incorporating an escrow function at the heart of its process, and thus guaranteeing its ability to fulfill its customers' pay requests, Taobao built confidence into the very idea of e-commerce. Supported by a nationwide advertising campaign, and further assisted by eBay's decision not to adapt its American-developed Web site to the needs and tastes of the Chinese, Taobao took off. By the end of 2006, its share of China's C2C market had risen from 8 percent to nearly 70 percent, and eBay had pulled out of the country. Defending its home territory, the Yangtze crocodile had comprehensively seen off the American shark—and Jack Ma was on his way to building an empire that would reach every person in China with Internet access.

Today, Ma's payment system, now known as Alipay, is responsible for processing half of all online transactions in China. It processes more than half a trillion dollars annually—five times more than the country's second-biggest system, Tencent's Tenpay, and over 20 times more than China UnionPay, the state-owned body with a monopoly over China's bank card authorization network. Ma's original business, Alibaba.com, is today the world's biggest business-to-business (B2B) online trading platform, facilitating sales between millions of small and medium-sized enterprises from more than 240 countries. Its business, however, is dwarfed by the advertising and commission revenues earned by Taobao and Alibaba's other leading consumer-oriented Web site, Tmall, the country's busiest online shopping mall, which Ma launched in 2008 to host listings by retailers and brand owners.

"WE WANT TO BE NUMBER ONE"

How did Jack Ma pull this off? After all, not only was he from a family with no business background, but by the age of 35, all Ma had to show for his life was one failed Web site. He had been born in the eastern Chinese city of Hangzhou in 1964 to parents who were both *pingtan* artists: storytellers who used a mixture of narrative and song to tell traditional stories. One of the biggest struggles of Ma's early years was simply getting into university. After eventually finding a place at the Hangzhou Teachers' Institute, he graduated in 1988 with a degree in English. By the mid 1990s, after a few years teaching English, among other jobs, he found work as an interpreter. In 1995, on a trip to Seattle as an interpreter for a trade delegation, he experienced the Internet for the first time. The Web browser had been invented just three years before, and Google did not yet exist. Web search engines were largely limited to indexing titles and headlines, not the full text of Web pages. Searching the Web for information about China, Ma found almost nothing. Sensing an opportunity, he borrowed $2,000 and launched China Pages, a business information Web site featuring an indexed list of Chinese companies interested in finding overseas buyers for their goods. At a time when China's total Internet user base numbered less than 1 million, the business, not surprisingly, attracted little interest, and closed within two years.

But Ma had seen enough to know he was onto something. In early 1999, he gathered 18 people in his Hangzhou apartment and pitched them an idea for an e-commerce business that would use the Internet to connect Chinese manufacturers, especially smaller ones, with potential buyers around the world. Ma, using his now legendary ability to convince others to back him, persuaded the group to commit $60,000 to his venture after just two hours of discussion. Alibaba was born.

Soon, he was telling everyone who would listen about the potential of his idea. "We don't want to be number one in China. We want to be number one in the world," he told Hong Kong's *South China Morning Post* newspaper a few months later, when his total staff count was still less than 20. Within a year he had secured further support from crucial sources. First, he brought on board Joe Tsai, a Taiwanese lawyer with rich experience in investment. Then, using Tsai's connections, he persuaded Goldman Sachs to buy 23 percent of the company for $5 million, and Japan's Softbank to buy 31 percent for $20 million, which gave Alibaba enough money to tide it over the tough period that followed the bursting of the dotcom bubble. With China's accession to the World Trade Organization in late 2001, Ma saw Alibaba move into the black as buyers around the world started looking to source ever more goods from China.

In late 2007, four years after launching Taobao and establishing Alipay, Ma successfully listed Alibaba.com in Hong Kong, raising $1.5 billion and briefly earning it a $26 billion valuation. Its fortunes then fell as trade declined worldwide in the recession that followed the global financial crisis. By then, however, it had long been clear that consumer-oriented e-commerce was replacing Alibaba's original B2B as its driving force. Once the company had seen off eBay, it poured resources into Taobao, Tmall, and a string of smaller e-commerce businesses. The group as a whole became profitable in 2009, and net earnings have soared ever since. With China's e-commerce market forecast to increase fivefold to around 10 trillion yuan (about $1.63 trillion) by 2020, it is hard to see a future in which Alibaba's revenues and profits cannot accelerate further.

MA TAKES ON THE BANKS

Having secured his dominance of China's e-commerce business, Jack Ma focused his attention on fulfilling his global ambitions. Ahead of the company's New York listing in 2014, Alibaba embarked on an acquisition spree, buying up businesses both in China and overseas. Most, such as its investments in building a logistics consortium, were clearly rooted in extending its current business, as orders placed through Alibaba Web sites account for around 70 percent of all package deliveries in China. But the steps Ma is taking to establish Alibaba as a financial force stand out as having the furthest potential reach.

In 2008, frustrated by the failure of China's state-owned banks to support small and medium-sized private enterprises, Ma declared, "If banks don't change, we will change banks." The following year, building on Alipay's success, he set up a finance arm to make small loans to Alibaba.com users. A borrower's creditworthiness was gauged using two key metrics: the total value of business it conducted through Alibaba.com and the ratings it received from its customers. Despite an average loan value of less than $10,000, by early 2014, Alibaba's total loan book stood at $2 billion, with less than 2 percent nonperforming.

As with its e-commerce Web sites, this experiment in B2B was followed up by a consumer-directed play. Much as Taobao rapidly grew to become several times greater than Alibaba.com, so Alibaba's consumer finance arm has overtaken its loans to small business, except even faster and more dramatically.

Alibaba only entered consumer finance in mid 2013, launching a money-market product called Yu'e Bao ("extra treasure"). To open one of these accounts, all any person needed was an Alipay account, and once opened, they could freely deposit and withdraw money at any time. What made Yu'e Bao attractive was that it offered savers a markedly better return than the notoriously low rates offered by China's banks. A year after its launch, some 100 million people had opened Yu'e Bao accounts, depositing the equivalent of $93 billion. According to Reuters, Yu'e Bao's arrival, followed shortly after by similar products from China's two other Internet giants, Baidu and Tencent, resulted in total personal deposits at China's leading banks falling more than 1 trillion yuan ($160 billion).

While it is inconceivable that Ma could push aside China's massively powerful state-owned banks and rise to dominate finance in the way he sits astride e-commerce, he certainly could play a big role in making the country's financial system far more market-oriented than it now is. Though personal financial services can be highly controlled by the government, in actuality it's a gray area in terms of regulatory intensity in China—and financial officials have been willing so far to allow Alibaba to continue running Yu'e Bao. This suggests they are happy with the effect competition is having in helping them move toward the government's long-stated goal of interest-rate liberalization.

THE JUMP STRATEGY

Identifying where Jack Ma's business genius lies in all this is not easy. Certainly, he doesn't attribute it to meticulous planning. As far back as the late 1990s, he said: "If you plan, you lose. If you don't plan, you win." Some of his most audacious moves have been highly opportunistic. Taobao, for example, was set up in reaction to eBay's arrival, not as a result of blue-sky thinking, with Alipay hastily assembled to make sure it worked.

But Alibaba's strategy is not opportunism pure and simple. Rather, it is a form of opportunism that draws on a vision—one initially based in an awareness of the Internet's potential to link businesses and people to each other, which has since expanded to include the idea of combining the Internet's reach with the capabilities developed inside Alibaba to enter new areas of business.

Zeng Ming, Alibaba's chief strategy officer, puts it this way: "Alibaba isn't following the traditional business strategy of having a core competence. Instead it's constantly looking for the right combination of opportunity and competence—where we can bring together the biggest opportunity and the most important leverage point. We don't jump randomly, we do this in a very disciplined way."

Exactly how disciplined is debatable; even the best companies rely on hunches and luck from time to time, especially when they have to cope with an economy as fast-changing as China's. Moreover, many other companies in China use very similar "jump" strategies to enter markets beyond their existing arena in search of new sources of growth. First, they rapidly take measure of a changing business environment, then they develop the capabilities needed to move into it. We'll explore this further in the next two chapters. For now, however, I want to look at a third element that Jack Ma and his cohorts share: that intangible but nonetheless real force that motivates entrepreneurs in China to found and drive companies able to search out and seize opportunities that I call China's entrepreneurial spirit.

BREACHING THE DAM

The entrepreneurial spirit now manifesting itself across China has numerous origins, some extending back centuries. These include the country's long history of trade and great invention (especially the four "great" discoveries of papermaking, printing, the compass, and gunpowder), and the justifiable pride that

Chinese people have in their long-standing scientific and technological influence. But if you want to single out one source of the energy that has released a succession of entrepreneurial waves across China, you don't need to go so far back in history. You need only look to the four-decade-long blockade on innovation and intellectual growth that Mao Zedong created during his years running China.

When the Communist Party established the People's Republic of China in 1949, it returned order to a country that for more than a century had suffered from Western imperial incursions, a Japanese invasion, civil wars, and famines. That order, however, came at a high cost. Mao's view of order was based on a system that did not allow anyone to visibly excel at the expense of others, except through the Communist Party. Free-form entrepreneurship was not just exploitative, but contrary to the notion of how the world was supposed to work. To reinforce this, Mao launched a series of disastrous political movements (including the Cultural Revolution of the late 1960s and early 1970s). These efforts claimed tens of millions of lives, blocked all individual aspirations, and stultified the Chinese economy.

Following Mao's death in 1976, his successors recognized that his repressive policies could not be sustained, even if they wanted to see them continue. A five-day meeting of the Communist Party's Central Committee in December 1978 led to the release of energy pent up in the preceding decades. Gathered at a hotel in west Beijing, the committee agreed to allow experimental economic reforms that would tentatively allow market forces once again to operate in China. The primary leader of this reform movement was Deng Xiaoping, chairman of the party's Central Advisory Committee. Deng had been in party leadership positions since the 1960s, always advocating for (and sometimes overseeing) economic reforms. He had been targeted and pushed aside during the Cultural Revolution, but with Mao's death he and his ideas returned to ascendancy, and he became the de facto leader of the country.

The first reforms under this new regime took place in the countryside. Under what became known as the "Household Responsibility System," farmers, once they had met various contractual obligations to sell a share of their produce to the state, were free to sell everything else they grew or raised at whatever price they could find on the market. After years of repression, agricultural output soared, rising by as much as 10 percent *annually* through the 1980s. For the first time in decades, everyone had enough food on their tables.

Further reforms continued through the decade. First in a handful of "special economic zones," then at other locations along the coast, foreign enterprises, mostly small-scale export-processing operations from Hong Kong, opened factories and processing plants. An increasing number of goods were sold at market-set prices, not state-set ones. Then, in April 1988, with the National People's Congress, China's parliament approved an amendment to the country's constitution granting private companies the formal right to exist.

Even before formal legal recognition, hundreds of thousands of private businesses had already started up. In Fujian, farmer Xu Lianjie and his partner Sze Man Bok spotted an opportunity to improve women's lives and started a business making sanitary napkins, subsequently naming it Hengan. In central China, engineer Ren Zhengfei left the army and moved to Shenzhen to found a firm, Huawei, that bought used office telecommunications equipment from Hong Kong for use in mainland China. In Beijing, a group of engineers from the Chinese Academy of Sciences established Legend, the precursor to the modern computing giant Lenovo, to import televisions. And in Taizhou in Zhejiang Province, 23-year-old Li Shufu established his first business, a refrigerator components firm, paving the way for his motorcycle and car-making business, Geely, in the following decade.

By the late 1980s, however, China's initial period of reform was in trouble. The decade's initial burst of growth gave way to a sharp rise in inflation and growing unease over official corruption, which in turn spilled over into widespread protests, including Beijing's student-led democracy movement. Following the suppression of those protests in Tiananmen Square and elsewhere around the country in June 1989, most of China's leaders advocated a rolling back of reforms and a return to a centrally controlled economy.

The exception was Deng Xiaoping. While he was as intent as anyone on maintaining the Communist Party's grip on China's political life, he believed strongly that only further reforms could guarantee China's continued economic development. So in January and February 1992, at the age of 88, he went on his now legendary six-week "southern tour"—first to Shenzhen, which had already established itself as an export-processing boomtown just across the border from Hong Kong, and then to Shanghai, calling on officials to resume his policies of market liberalization and opening China to the world.

His trip was the catalyst for the change that has propelled China to where it is today. It launched a second wave of entrepreneurial energy, one that both lifted those companies established in the 1980s and led to the launching of a second wave of entrepreneurs. This generation of business leaders was so large that its members are often referred to as the "Gang of '92," after the year in which many of them started out.

Many of the leading entrepreneurs from this period left secure jobs in government or academia to *xia hai* or "jump into the sea" of business—nowhere more so than in Beijing, where conservative pressures had made life stifling inside official organizations. These people saw themselves as escaping a safe but stultifying life as bureaucrats and gaining the freedom and rewards of entrepreneurship along with the risk. One of the best-known members of the Gang of '92 is Chen Dongsheng. Today the chairman of Taikang Life Insurance, China's biggest private insurer, he left a position at the Development Research Center of the State Council, an offshoot of China's cabinet, to set up his first company, China Guardian Auction Company. Outside China, Huang Nubo, a former official at the Communist Party's propaganda department, is perhaps the most controversial of this wave. A billionaire thanks to the success of his property firm Beijing Zhongkuan, he achieved worldwide fame in 2011 when he offered $8 million to buy a 300-square-kilometer chunk of Iceland, leading to accusations that he was trying to establish a strategic foothold for China in the North Atlantic.

My favorite origin story from the Gang of '92 is that of Feng Lun. After graduating with an economics degree from Northwestern University in the city of Xian, he worked as a lecturer at the Marxism and Leninism Research Institute of the Communist Party's Central Party School in Beijing—the Communist Party's top ideological training body. In the wake of June 1989, however, due to its association with figures sympathetic to the student protestors, Feng's department was closed. He moved to

Hainan, China's southernmost province and traditionally a place where disgraced officials were sent into exile as punishment.

There, on a subtropical island 1,500 miles from Beijing's grim political climate, Feng found himself in the middle of a spectacular property boom. As speculative money flooded in from across China, Hainan's GDP growth rate leapt to an astonishing 42 percent in 1992, and Feng abandoned his official post to start a property firm (or, as he told me recently, "I decided to move outside of the system").

Toward the end of the following year, finance officials reined in Hainan's overheated economy, popping its property bubble and sending the island into a recession whose aftermath would linger well into the 2000s. But Feng had sensed the tightening in advance, and rapidly relocated back to Beijing before the recession hit. Back in Beijing, his company, Vantone Holdings, became one of China's most successful real estate development companies. It has also been one of the few to build a successful international business. Its overseas operations include leasing six floors of New York's rebuilt World Trade Center to house a business center for Chinese companies looking to invest in the United States.

CHINA OPENS ITS DOORS

Through the 1990s, these two waves of entrepreneurs—the pioneers of the 1980s and the Gang of '92—found themselves operating in a business environment more open to the outside world than at any time in China's recent history. The government invited multinationals into the country, guiding them wherever possible into joint-venture partnerships and encouraging them to share their technology with local firms in return for access to the China market. Significant numbers of Chinese started going overseas to study, work, or just see the world. The numbers were small compared with today, but those trips would have major repercussions, none more than Jack Ma's encounter with the Internet during his 1995 visit to Seattle.

Much of the decade was spent in experimentation and learning. In Qingdao, Haier began adding scale to its operations while continuing to develop its brand identity. In Shenzhen, Huawei explored how to sell its telecom equipment to less-well-off provincial operators away from the coast. And in Taizhou, Li Shufu started wondering whether he would be able to transfer the knowledge acquired making motorcycles to car production.

Even as the economy boomed, there was also a growing awareness that if China were to close the gap with the developed world, it was going to need further reforms. No one stressed this more than the second most important single figure in shaping China's economy after Deng Xiaoping: Zhu Rongji, the country's premier from 1998 to 2003.

Zhu's message was uncompromising. For China to succeed, Chinese companies would have to be able to compete with the best, and the only way that could happen would be if barriers to such competition were pulled down, regardless of the consequences for those enterprises unable to cope. Through the late 1990s, he oversaw the closing or merger of hundreds of thousands of poorly performing state-owned enterprises, which led to tens of millions of people losing their jobs. Then, in the early 2000s, Zhu pushed China into the World Trade Organization. The market-opening measures that followed saw foreign inflows more than double and exports embark on their relentless rise, which would see China become the world's biggest exporter in 2009 and its biggest trader by 2013. In the space of one decade, the country went from a respectable middleweight with an economy the size of Italy's to a major international power with an economy second in size only to the United States's. During this period, China's consumer markets went from having potential to being real. Car sales in 2000 were 1.2 million; they rose 11-fold, to 13.8 million, by 2010, with China displacing the United States as the world's biggest car market in the process. Mobile phone users increased from 85 million to 800 million over the decade, and Internet users went from just over 20 million to more than 450 million.

Wherever you looked, the numbers were astonishing. Perhaps the biggest and most far-reaching market development was the creation from scratch of a nation of homeowners. Toward the end of the 1990s, housing was still provided through a person's "work unit"—the enterprise or other organization they worked for—and hardly any urban residents owned their homes. As of 2014, thanks to a radical program of privatization that allowed almost everyone to buy their apartments at a hugely discounted price, around 85 percent of urban families lived in homes they owned.

This establishment of an urban housing market paved the way for the growth of a series of gigantic property firms, creating numerous billionaires along the way. Among them are Wang Jianlin of Dalian Wanda, the country's biggest property group, Hui Ka Yan of Guangzhou-based Evergrande Real Estate, and husband-and-wife couple Pan Shiyi and Zhang Xin of SOHO China, the country's largest office real estate developer. The housing market was also the major driver of China's markets for furniture, appliances, electronic goods, home decor products, and all the other things people need to make their homes habitable— explaining, in large part, how Haier managed to become the world's biggest large-appliance maker.

China's liftoff through the 2000s floated all boats. Even the state-owned sectors thrived. Industries like telecoms, power, aviation, and petrochemicals were freed of their worst performers, thanks to Zhu's cull of the late 1990s. They saw a strong rise in revenues, profitability, and return on assets.

But despite those gains, it was also becoming clear that China's future would eventually lie with its private companies. Riding the country's tide of economic growth, a third wave of entrepreneurs established and grew their businesses, most prominently its Internet companies, as Tencent, founded in 1998 by Pony Ma, and Baidu, founded in 2000 by Robin Li, established themselves alongside Alibaba. Overall, the private sector's share of China's total capital investment rose from less than one-quarter in the late 1990s to nearly two-thirds in the late 2000s. While profitability at state-owned enterprises rose, it never matched the level of private companies. For those willing to look, a new era was taking shape.

It was during this third entrepreneurial wave that I began to study Chinese entrepreneurs in depth. In 2005, I published an article in *strategy+business* called "China's Five Surprises," in which I described the mind-set and momentum of the up-and-coming business builders whom I knew:

One question is in the mind of every fledgling entrepreneur in the high-tech startups of Beijing's Zhongguancun neighborhood, the fabrication hubs of Wenzhou, the industrial region of Dalian, and dozens of other Chinese business centers: "Why not me?" Success is all around them. . . . Young Chinese businesspeople are driven by materialistic desires, eager to "catch up" with the rest of the world, and almost giddy with a sense of multiplying opportunity. They have read Internet chronicles of the triumphs of Yahoo, Silicon Graphics, and Google. They see themselves as the creators of the world's future Intels, Apples, and Microsofts, and some of them probably will be.

That same year, Baidu had its Nasdaq IPO, generating front-page acclaim in the Chinese press. The momentum was so strong among entrepreneurs, it felt as if holes had been punched in a steam pipe that had been building up pressure for a long time. After growing up on a steady diet of two ideas—"Life is good under communism" and "Acceptable behavior is determined by the authority of the parent, boss, and leader as outlined by Confucius"—this third generation of entrepreneurs began to carve out their own rules. Figures such as Jack Ma, Pony Ma, and Robin Li never questioned China's system as such, but they moved beyond it rapidly, displaying a sense of self-assurance, as if they felt entitled to succeed, that would have been impossible to imagine in the previous two generations. They backed up this confidence with a high-speed energy and agility that kept them one step ahead of constraints. To circumvent rules barring foreign companies from holding stakes in Chinese Internet firms, they created new forms of legal entity that would allow them to list in the United States and other overseas markets. That brought them access to foreign capital—and also brought in foreign expertise. And they specialized in moving very fast, allowing them to bring services such as instant messaging or online payments to hundreds of millions of users before China's state-owned telecom operators or financial institutions had even started thinking seriously about how such businesses could undermine their own offerings.

YET ANOTHER WAVE

Now there is a fourth wave of Chinese disruptors: members of the entrepreneurial generation born from the 1980s on, who never experienced Mao Zedong's regime firsthand.

These are people who have spent their entire life in China's economic-reform era. They have known only a country whose economy has expanded year after year, and have no firsthand experience of the country's socialist era. Moreover, they were all born after China's introduction of its single-child family policy in 1979. They are thus almost all only children without siblings. Often referred to as Little Emperors, their generation is widely regarded as having received too much care and attention from parents and grandparents growing up. Members of the post-1980s generation are almost universally far better educated than their predecessors. Many have been educated overseas or gained work experience at multinational companies. Even those who have not tend to have a more worldly outlook thanks to having been raised during China's opening and due to their exposure to the Internet in particular.

Whereas their parents' generation tended to build businesses

Anything Is Possible

through trial and error, many members of this generation have far greater exposure to business ideas and thinking from the start. For some, this comes from being raised to inherit their parents' businesses. Kelly Zong, for example, has long been groomed to take over the reins at Hangzhou Wahaha Group, China's largest beverage maker, from her father, Zong Qinghou, another of China's top 10 richest figures. Born in 1982, Kelly Zong attended high school and university in California before returning to China to work for Wahaha in the mid 2000s. She has already publicly criticized the traditionally close relationship between companies and officials as a source of bribery, and said she will replace her father's top-down management style with a more participatory, team-based approach. It's evident that her plans for running the company already look very different from her father's way of doing things.

Many of the start-ups now being established by fourth-wave entrepreneurs are Internet-based, using the tools made available by companies such as Alibaba and Tencent to build e-commerce businesses. Their owners are clearly trying to ape the successes not just of American Internet companies, such as Google and Facebook, but also of China's homegrown giants, the BATs.

Though this latest generation has yet to produce any businesses on the scale of an Alibaba or Tencent, it has produced some possible contenders. Wang Xing, for example, sold his first successful business, Xiaonei, a social media Web site modeled on Facebook, for several million dollars in 2005 at age 26. Subsequently renamed Renren, it was floated by its new owners on the New York Stock Exchange in 2011, raising $584 million. It briefly was China's fourth-largest Internet company by market capitalization, behind Tencent, Baidu, and Alibaba.

If Wang Xing had stayed with Xiaonei into its Renren years, he might have made millions more. But he says he has no regrets about selling the company when he did, not just because Renren's fortunes have since fallen (both revenues and users dropped sharply in 2013), but because he had other things to move on to. His next hit was Fanfou.com, an online messaging service similar to Twitter. For a short time, Fanfou.com was China's most popular online messaging service, until the government suspended it in the wake of a series of riots involving Uyghurs, one of China's largest Muslim ethnic populations, in the country's restive western Xinjiang region in 2009. Undeterred, Wang then launched Meituan.com, a group discount Web site similar to Groupon. Now 10 percent owned by Alibaba, transactions through its site were worth $2.5 billion in 2013, and were expected to more than double to $6.4 billion in 2014.

A SHARED VISION

There are differences between the generations, but these should not be exaggerated. Many entrepreneurs who founded companies in the 1980s, for example, had less formal education than those who followed them, and almost none had any experience in business when they started out. Even today, they can remain a little rough-edged. At my most recent meeting with Xu Lianjie, the founder of Hengan International, in the boardroom of his company headquarters in Fujian on a damp late-winter morning, he was wrapped up against the cold in four layers of jackets and zipped-up pullovers.

Similarly unconcerned about public perceptions of his personal behavior, Huawei's founder, Ren Zhengfei, for most of his career shunned the media, believing that his company's track record could speak for itself. This so-called secretive behavior hurt perceptions of his company overseas. Ren ended up changing his policy in late 2013. In a series of interviews with Western and Chinese journalists clearly aimed at showing a more rounded picture of his personality, he talked about his modest upbringing by school-teacher parents and his enjoyment of drinking tea and reading.

Few of those first-generation entrepreneurs, back in the 1980s, could have imagined what might lie ahead. In 1984, Liu Chuanzhi gathered 10 of his engineering colleagues at the Chinese Academy of Sciences' Institute of Computing Technology to start a business importing televisions, ponderously known as the Chinese Academy of Sciences Computer Technology Research Institute New Technology Development Company. Only 30 years later, that business, now called Lenovo, is the world's largest seller of personal computers.

And as well as possessing a pioneering spirit, many also showed great courage in starting businesses less than a decade after the end of the Cultural Revolution, when people were pilloried or even killed for having had a capitalist past.

Many members of the second generation, represented by Chen Dongsheng and other entrepreneurs from the Gang of '92 who left official posts to start businesses, like to portray themselves as the most serious of China's entrepreneurs. They see themselves as bearing responsibilities to society beyond running a successful business. But plenty of their predecessors, such as Broad Group's founder Zhang Yue, and those who started businesses later, most publicly Jack Ma, have also come to see themselves as important spokespeople on China's future trajectory.

And though Ma and all those others who started their businesses from around 2000 onward may appear more questioning of established practices than their predecessors, they also willingly continue working within China's current institutional framework. "Their love of their country isn't the same as that of the generation before them," says Taikang Life Insurance's chief, Chen Dongsheng. "But those born in the 1980s and '90s may in fact see China more positively. As I see it, because they were raised at a time when they could see China undergoing such great development, and because they didn't have any memories of how China was in the 1950s and '60s, they approve of the Communist Party rather than oppose it."

Members of the third and fourth generations from the 2000s and 2010s generally combine opportunism with pragmatism. They try to avoid business areas where state-owned companies are strongly entrenched, preferring instead to find areas where they have greater freedom to operate without official oversight. But as we'll see in subsequent chapters, these younger entrepreneurs often find themselves aligned with those parts of the government that are liberalizing the economy. Further, the more success that these third- and fourth-generation entrepreneurs achieve, the more likely the government is to extend further its market reforms.

A SHARED SPIRIT

At the heart of China's entrepreneurial spirit lie three core elements: pride, ambition, and a shared cultural heritage.

Pride is the most straightforward of these elements. "Chinese

Table 1: Four Decades of Entrepreneurs

Era	Characteristics	Entreprenuer/company (year of establishment)
1980s	The typical business of this era was the *getihu*, or individually owned business. Most of the businesses listed in the next column, though established in the 1980s, date their success to the 1990s. Many of the entrepreneurs of this generation had little or even no formal education beyond high school, and almost none had experience in business when they started, a background many of them like to stress even today.	Zhang Ruimin/Haier (1984*) Wang Shi/Vanke (1984) Liu Chuanzhi/Lenovo (formerly Legend) (1984) Wei Jianjun/Great Wall Motors (1984) Xu Lianjie/Hengan International (1985) Liang Wengen/Sany (1986) Li Shufu/Zhejiang Geely (1986) Zhang Yue/Broad Group (1988) Ren Zhengfei/Huawei (1988) Wang Jianlin/Dalian Wanda (1988) Zong Qinghou/Hangzhou Wahaha Group (1988)
1990s	Launched by Deng Xiaoping's 1992 "Southern Tour" to Shenzhen and Shanghai, which he undertook to relaunch economic reform, many of the entrepreneurs of this generation left posts in government or academia to "jump into the sea" of business. Typically far more educated than their predecessors from the 1980s, many of the leading entrepreneurs from this period see themselves as bearers of wider responsibilities to China and society that extend well beyond business.	Feng Lun, Vantone Holdings (1991) Guo Guangchang/Fosun (1992) Wang Wei/SF Express (1993) Chen Dongsheng/China Guardian Auction (1993), Taikang Life Insurance (1996) Huang Nubo/Zhongkun Group (1995) Zhang Jindong/Suning (1996)
Early–mid 2000s	The key turning point for this generation was China's entry into the World Trade Organization in December 2001 and the opening of China's markets that followed. Almost all of China's leading Internet companies date from this period. Entrepreneurs who started out in the 2000s are typically more internationally minded than their predecessors, often drawing their inspiration from companies in other parts of the world.	Pony Ma/Tencent (1998) Liu Qiangdong/JD.com (1998) Charles Chao/Sina (1998) Jack Ma/Alibaba (1999) Robin Li/Baidu (2000) Diane Wang/DHgate (2004) Zhou Hongyi/Qihoo (2005) Wang Jingbo/Noah Asset Management (2005) Victor Koo/Youku (2006)
Late 2000s–2010s	Many of China's latest generation of entrepreneurs are launching businesses aimed at combining the potential offered by the Internet, especially the mobile Internet, with the new consumer class that has formed on the back of China's economic resurgence. Those born in the 1980s, or even in some cases the 1990s, and raised as single children only know reform-era China. Members of this generation are widely regarded as having a more relaxed attitude about business than their predecessors, less worried about failure or surrendering ownership of their companies to outside investors. Many have experience in life overseas and, thanks to growing up in an Internet-connected world, are aware of global trends, especially technological ones.	Yu Gang/Yihaodian (2008) Wang Xing/Meituan (2010) Eric Shen/Vipshop (2010) Lei Jun/Xiaomi (2011)

*1984 was the year Zhang Ruimin joined Haier, then called the Qingdao Refrigerator Factory. The company's origins formally date back to the 1920s.

entrepreneurs see an important part of their mission as playing a major role in the achievement of national prosperity," says Diane Wang, the founder of DHgate.com, a company that, like Alibaba.com, links Chinese businesses with buyers around the world. Seeing their country once again achieve the kind of national greatness it has enjoyed for much of its history is a key motivator for the Chinese people. They are acutely aware of the country's achievements, and also of the weaknesses that saw it fall so far back during much of the 19th and 20th centuries.

Wang herself is a good example. She began her career as a teacher at Tsinghua University, one of China's top three universities. Then she went to work for Microsoft and Cisco, before becoming CEO of China's first big online bookstore, Joyo.com—one of the several businesses set up by smartphone maker Xiaomi's Lei Jun. After Lei sold Joyo (now known as Amazon.cn) to Amazon for $75 million in 2004, Wang left the company, had a baby, and launched DHgate.

From the start, she was determined that her business would take a global view—a mission reflected in its name, which derives its first two initials from Dunhuang, a city in northwest China that was once an important crossroads on the Silk Road. "The Chinese are very proud of the Silk Road and its role as a global trade route when China was at its most powerful. Today, thanks in part to the Internet era, we think China again has a chance of regaining a similar glory," she says.

Closely related to this pride is the second strand in China's entrepreneurial spirit, ambition, and an increasing desire to aim for the highest goals. Some of this ambition is directed at creating companies that can see off their international rivals both in China and around the world—which means doing things that no other business has done before. Zhang Ruimin, for example, having built Haier into a world leader, now harbors other ambitions outside of being a market winner.

One of his goals is to close the gap between Haier and its customers, so they can buy the goods they want directly from Haier through a Web site. Already, he says, the company has a specific final customer identified for one in five of the products on its production lines.

Zhang is also deeply involved in an ongoing campaign to restructure Haier and make it into a company where every element is entrepreneurial and every employee regards him or herself as an entrepreneur. His effort to do this has centered on organizing Haier's staff into approximately 4,000 small teams, each of which operates like a small business in its own right. The vast majority of these teams are product-based, making and selling Haier's goods. A small number handle specific functions, such as human resources or financial planning, and an even smaller number look after the company's overall strategic direction, overseeing the creation of new teams for new products or the closure of teams which no longer serve any need.

The different teams contract with each other to ensure access to the services and skills they need. They each choose their own leaders, and have the right to replace them if they feel they are underperforming. How much they are paid depends on their performance.

Zhang says his goal is to turn Haier into an "ecosphere": an organization in which many people have decision-making power, and those at higher levels are only responsible for setting the overall master direction.

One of the words that run through all his discussions of Haier's future direction is *platform,* by which he means the base from which the company's teams operate. "Now, Haier doesn't authorize employees to do their work. Instead, we provide a platform for them. We are committed to providing the platform, in which there are different kinds of businesses. Some of these are existing ones that need to be transformed, others are new ones that need to be set up."

This reorganization is very much at its early stages, but already is having a major impact. In 2013, Haier laid off 16,000 staff members, almost all of them non-customer-facing mid-level management or administrative employees. Another 10,000 were due to follow in 2014. Among those fired have been some long-serving figures. "We just fired an employee this month who had been working at Haier for 20 years in charge of sales of white household appliances across China," says Zhang. "He left Haier because he couldn't drive innovation or launch start-up businesses."

The firing came as a shock to many staff at Haier. Like Zhang's destruction of a refrigerator 30 years ago, though, it has served as a call to action. His view of business—that in today's environment a company must be continually transforming itself to stay in step with the times—is shared by many of China's most successful entrepreneurs. Indeed, Zhang's compulsion to drive his company from one transformation to the next is anything but a rarity in China. In the last two decades, a body of immensely talented and driven business leaders has arisen who see their mission in broadly similar terms: less in terms of success, but more in terms of creating companies "of their times." "In the past, the management of Chinese companies was really simple," Zhang told me in mid 2014. "All we had to do was learn from Japanese or American companies. But now, we have no example to reference, especially in the reform of large companies." The task of coming up with innovative, unprecedented ways of doing things falls to him.

Business ambition is only part of what motivates China's entrepreneurs. Through countless conversations with business leaders from all industries and of all ages, I know that, almost without exception, running a successful business is merely a starting point. Particularly since the mid 2000s, many of China's entrepreneurs have seen the enormous impact their activities have had on China. As they have remade the ways in which people live their daily lives, most want to have an impact beyond their immediate business.

If there is one thing shown by the experiences of Jack Ma and his peers—Pony Ma at Tencent, Haier's Zhang Ruimin, Huawei's Ren Zhengfei, and many others—it is that in today's China, extreme ambition can pay off handsomely. As their businesses have advanced, so the possibilities open before them have kept expanding. It would only seem rational to conclude that they too can harbor ambitions to play a central role in such areas as energy, transport, communications, and construction.

How far can they take their ambitions? In January 2013, Jack Ma told Alibaba staff he would be stepping down as CEO later that year to broaden his personal goals and take on China's biggest problem, the disastrous state of its environment. As he noted in a blog posting shortly thereafter, "Alibaba was founded with a simple mission to help small business owners make money. But our next challenge is to join forces with the people of China and beyond to build an ecosystem that can help even more people make a decent living and push for change that benefits everyone."

Such concerns were put to the side while Ma, as Alibaba's chairman, engineered Alibaba's share listing in New York. With that task now completed, and Alibaba's revenues and profits continuing to rise strongly, he is expected to return to his broader ambitions.

Few entrepreneurs harbor aspirations as far-reaching as Ma's, but as one of a handful of people who, in less than one generation, "revolutionized how Chinese people live, learn, work and play," he has firsthand experience of just what is possible.

While the nature of the pride and ambition in the Chinese entrepreneurial spirit can explain much of the drive to succeed that keeps its leading entrepreneurs pushing forward, a third strand explains the purpose of their drive, arising from China's Confucian heritage.

At the heart of Confucian thought is the idea that for the world to be well ordered, people must behave properly and fulfill their prescribed roles. It follows from this, therefore, that rulers and others with power have a duty to govern well. It is their duty to instill order into the world.

Much of the subtlety and interest in Confucian thought is in teasing out exactly what is right behavior and how this can be encouraged or enforced. The point that I want to stress, however, is that ruling is principally about intervention and not about allowing matters to find a natural balance.

At one level, their having been raised in such a tradition points to why China's entrepreneurs often appear to have a paternal approach to running their businesses, ensuring order via a top-down management style. But on another, deeper level, Chinese leaders tend to harbor an underlying assumption that the natural tendency of the world is to run toward disorder. Control is always necessary.

Two consequences relevant to China's entrepreneurial spirit follow from this. First has been a centuries-long rejection of free-market economics and related streams of Western thought. Many Westerners believe that the world, if left to its own devices, will find a natural order of its own—and that this is especially true of markets and other economic systems. The Chinese tend to believe that markets, like all complex systems, require constant monitoring and supervision in order to deliver their best results. Given the country's long history of sophisticated domestic and international commerce, much of which coincided with China also being the world's most advanced and sophisticated economy, the belief that market order requires the continual intervention of officials is deeply embedded in the national consciousness. Just as many Westerners are waiting for the inevitable moment when China drowns itself in sub-optimal command-and-control-style bureaucracy, many Chinese leaders take it for granted that the United States and other countries will render themselves impotent through cacophony and inefficiency.

The other consequence is that successful businesspeople, having prospered within a framework of order created by officials, feel a deep obligation to give their business purpose. It cannot just be about making money for themselves. The notion that a business should have a wider purpose from the start explains the widespread lack of interest in the trappings of wealth among most of the country's richest businesspeople. It also explains the idealist streak that has so often surfaced in my conversations with these entrepreneurs. "Social responsibility is a part of this," says Alibaba's chief strategy officer, Zeng Ming. "Faced with these kinds of historic opportunities, Jack [Ma] thinks it's our responsibility to make use of them."

While recently Ma has been the most publicly vocal advocate of China's facing up to the damage that has accompanied economic growth, he is far from alone. Nor is the state of China's environment their only concern. Zhang Yue, the CEO of Changsha-based air-conditioning and construction company Broad Group, has also emerged as a major figure advocating the adoption of economic policies aimed at making China's development ecologically sustainable. And Huang Nubo, the founder of Beijing-based property and resort developer Zhongkun, has raised concerns over the damage being done to China's social fabric by the rapid rate of its economic development. This, he points out, has led to both rising inequality and declining social mobility, especially for migrant workers who have left the countryside to find work in cities. "If you don't create channels for people to rise and don't tackle issues of fairness or a lack of legal knowledge, then you can create a society with a large underclass that's poor and a society that's unstable," he says.

Is this too idealistic a view of China's entrepreneurs? I would argue not. True, China is home to many businesspeople interested only in short-term gains or material success, who spend little or no time considering their country's immediate ills or longer-term prospects, or who are simply corrupt or criminal. Indeed, these may even be the majority. Yet, working in China since the early 1990s, I have repeatedly been struck by how many of the country's most successful entrepreneurs contribute much time and effort into social initiatives. They feel obliged to see their businesses as bearing broad responsibilities to society—especially compared to Western multinational companies with their commitment to shareholder return.

In this respect, I think China's top entrepreneurs embody the best elements of their country's culture. When China's most ambitious, driven, and talented young people look for role models, they find the most powerful examples among the ranks of those who have started companies, particularly in the Internet sector. Jack Ma, Pony Ma, Robin Li, and others like them are household names in China. China's markets, as they continue opening and expanding, are creating opportunities at an unprecedented rate for more entrepreneurs to join them and take similar roles themselves.

2

WIDE OPEN

Of all the entrepreneurs with global aspirations making headlines in China right now, the most casually flamboyant is forty-four-year-old Lei Jun. Often seen dressed in a black polo shirt and blue jeans, he helms Xiaomi, a company that makes low-cost, suspiciously iPhone-like smartphones. Perhaps unsurprisingly, he is often referred to in the business press as the Chinese Steve Jobs.

Is Xiaomi another low-end, knockoff enterprise, like the many others that have earned China a bad name in high-tech circles? Not quite. A few months after it was founded in mid 2010, it reached $1 billion in revenues faster than any other Chinese company before it. Despite serious competition not just from Apple and Samsung, but also Chinese heavyweights Lenovo and Huawei, Xiaomi hasn't slowed down. In 2013, it sold 15 million smartphones and acquired a valuation of $10 billion. Its initial target for 2014 was 40 million phones; after shipping more than

30 million units in the first half alone—giving it a global market share of 5 percent and pushing Samsung from its top spot as China's leading smartphone seller—that target was raised to 60 million. It eventually sold 61 million, allowing it to topple Samsung from its perch as China's leading smartphone vendor, and enough to push its valuation up to $40–$50 billion.

So far, almost all Xiaomi's sales have been in China, driven by a fan base of users as passionate about their phones as hard-core iPhone users are about theirs. Now the company is starting to move overseas. Branded Mi for international markets, Xiaomi is selling phones in Hong Kong, Singapore, Taiwan, the Philippines, and India. It plans to add another 10 countries, including Mexico, Brazil, and Russia.

Astonishing as Lei's achievement already is, Xiaomi is not his first major business success. Born in 1969 near Wuhan, an industrial city on the Yangtze river in central China, he graduated from Wuhan University in the late 1980s with a degree in computer science. Soon after, he moved to Shanghai to join Kingsoft, then the developer of China's top word-processing program. By 1998, he was the company's CEO. Over the next decade, he guided Kingsoft to a listing on the Hong Kong Stock Exchange while simultaneously launching a series of start-ups, including Joyo.com, the business he sold to Amazon, and YY, an online social platform for sharing videos that listed on the Nasdaq Stock Exchange in 2012 and was valued at $1.5 billion as of 2014.

It was no surprise, therefore, that Lei readily found backers when, along with a former Google engineer, Lin Bin, and five other partners, he set up Xiaomi in 2010 with the explicit goal of taking on Apple and its iPhone, first in China and ultimately in the rest of the world.

Like Apple, Xiaomi has no manufacturing facilities of its own, instead outsourcing all production to contract manufacturers such as Taiwan's Foxconn. But unlike Apple, which sells its products at a premium, Xiaomi sells its smartphones at just above cost. Its goal is to secure the greater part of its revenues from sales of software, services, advertising, and accessories—a strategy, as Lei likes to point out, that has more in common with Amazon than Apple. Unlike Amazon's, however, its phones are succeeding.

Further underlining the Amazon comparison, most of Xiaomi's sales are made online, either through its own Web site or through Sina Weibo, China's top microblogging platform, with more than 400 million registered users. Phones are typically sold in weekly batches ranging from a few thousand to a few hundred thousand units. Most batches sell out in a few hours, with new models sometimes going in just seconds. When Xiaomi announced its Red Rice smartphone in mid 2013—explicitly targeted to compete with Apple's lower-priced iPhone 5C, but with a $130 price tag that was less than one-quarter of its competitor's price—the company received more than 7 million pre-orders.

This direct sales model saves the company money on advertising and distribution, and also allows it direct contact with users. Every week it updates the Android-based user interface it uses for its phones, using suggestions sent in by fans. "Xiaomi is not selling a product, but an opportunity to participate," Lei told TechHive Web site journalist Michael Kan.

WHAT'S THE SECRET?

Rapid as Xiaomi's growth may be, it is not atypical for China. As we saw in the last chapter, since 2000, sales of consumer goods in almost every category have risen multiple-fold. Companies whose products reach even just a small proportion of the Chinese market have found themselves growing at hyperspeed, and sometimes generating fantastic returns.

This is a big change from the early 2000s, when many companies saw China as a country of great, but unrealized, potential. Indeed, ever since China opened itself up at the end of the 1970s—arguably, ever since the first efforts to penetrate the country's markets in the 19th century—foreign companies have come to China with the hope of selling their products to its massive population. The mid 2010s is the first time that this hope has been realized.

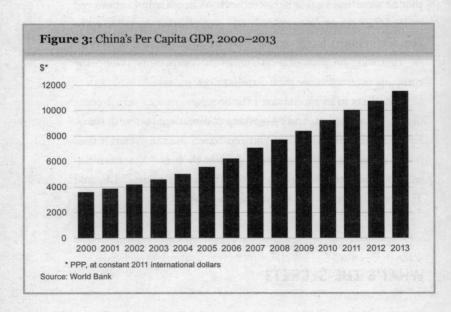

Figure 3: China's Per Capita GDP, 2000–2013

* PPP, at constant 2011 international dollars
Source: World Bank

It has taken longer than many people expected. They saw China's burgeoning prosperity and assumed broad-based consumption would rapidly follow. However, there was a whole series of reasons why it was difficult to sell goods in China before 2010, including a lack of infrastructure, a fragmented and largely inefficient group of logistics providers, a shortage of consumer credit, and, for many people, no way to pay for online purchases. Foreign companies recognized that, while the Chinese market clearly would be attractive in the future, the main reason for operating in the country was to produce goods for export to the rest of the world.

Now, all that has changed. To fully understand why China's consumer population can suddenly support so many successful entrepreneurial private companies, we need to look at the interplay among four factors propelling broad economic growth:

- Scale: The massive population within China, and the growing number of people who can afford a better life
- Openness: The continuing liberalization of the country's markets to private and foreign businesses
- Official support: The government's role in providing the physical and policy infrastructure needed for growth
- Technology: The impact of information and communications technology, particularly the Internet, in creating or offering access to new markets

These four factors can be combined into a simple formula: scale + openness + official support + technology = hyperfast growth of consumer markets.

Of the four components of this SOOT formula, scale is the easiest to recognize. It is generally understood that when per capita GDP reaches about $5,000, a tipping point is triggered, and the general population enters a consumer economy. The billion-person Chinese population crossed this threshold around 2005. Since then, per capita GDP has more than doubled. In addition, China's urbanization drive created hundreds of new city markets across the country. The scale of the Chinese consumer economy is now beyond any other country in the world.

The strength of a consumer market does not just depend on per capita wealth, however. Other factors must shift in ways that reinforce the power of the consumer market, or the scale won't matter. In China, all three of the other factors are shifting. Its markets are undergoing both a qualitative opening and a quantitative increase in value. Official policies that have long favored the state sector are switching to support private enterprise. Finally, technology is transforming the reach of business just as it is everywhere else in the world.

OPEN MARKETS

At the end of the 1970s, China had an almost totally closed, centrally planned economy. Today, many of its sectors are among the most open and liberalized in the world. Its consumer-goods, retail, and most manufacturing industries have few barriers to market entry or restrictions on ownership for either foreign or private Chinese companies. Even in those sectors where entrance remains controlled, such as finance and banking, energy, resources, telecom services, and media, restrictions are slowly easing—often, as we saw with Alibaba's moves into Internet finance in the last chapter, due to pressure from private companies.

As I noted in the last chapter, with incomes rising fast, not just in the richer coastal cities but also in lower-tier inland cities and even rural areas, demand for almost every category of goods has taken off. Companies wanting to sell into these markets have released an extraordinary number of products. For everything from soft drinks and snacks to consumer electronics and cars, China's population has an unrivaled choice.

As part of its efforts to switch the economy away from its reliance on foreign trade and investment, the government is actively encouraging people to consume more. In the wake of the global financial crisis, it subsidized purchases of home appliances in rural areas. In 2012, the Chinese government launched Consumption Promotion Month, a campaign that would run annually from April to May. And in 2013, it announced plans to make online sales account for at least 10 percent of retail sales nationwide. Its commerce ministry expects that, by 2015, China will have overtaken the United States to become the world's largest consumer market, with retail sales of more than $5 trillion. Soon, for any product or service you care to think of, China will be the biggest buyer—from tourism, where the 3 billion trips Chinese now take annually are expected to double in number by 2020, to the aircraft that will carry them, with both Boeing and Airbus forecasting a tripling of China's jet fleet by around 2030.

The huge numbers of Chinese moving into the middle class are exponentially greater than those of any other market. Research by Beijing-based economic research firm Gavekal Dragonomics sees China's total consumer population—those belonging to households with an income of $8,100 or more—rising from 350 million people in 2012 to 800 million by 2020.

Striking as these overall figures are, it's particularly noteworthy to consider the fastest-growing group within this total

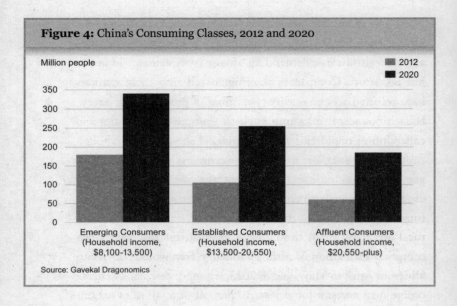

Figure 4: China's Consuming Classes, 2012 and 2020

Million people

2012
2020

Emerging Consumers (Household income, $8,100-13,500)
Established Consumers (Household income, $13,500-20,550)
Affluent Consumers (Household income, $20,550-plus)

Source: Gavekal Dragonomics

consumer population. The number of people in China's richest segment, those with household income of $20,550 or more, will more than triple, from 60 million to 185 million, within six years. Emerging consumers, those with a household income of $8,100 to $13,500, will grow from 180 million to 340 million, and established consumers, those with an income of $13,500 to $20,550, will increase from 105 million to around 255 million.

As this happens, there will be multiple shifts in consumption. Emerging consumers will start shopping in modern retail outlets, buying brand-name clothing or purchasing their food from supermarkets. Those moving up to the established consumer class will buy their first cars, while those in the affluent category will shift their purchases toward experiential products such as foreign travel.

Of course, spectacular as the opportunities created by open China are and will be, they must be qualified. As well as increasing in wealth, China's markets have also become more complex. The economy may be many times bigger than it was fifteen years ago, and its consumers may have much more spending power, but the country is anything but a single market. Rather, it is a collection of multiple, fragmented customer segments. Though the country's poorer inland and western regions have closed the gap on the coast in recent years, their richest cities still lag those of the eastern coast. Within any single province, wealth levels vary enormously. Even in the country's richest regions, such as the Pearl River delta in south China, the Yangtze River delta centered on Shanghai, and the Beijing-Tianjin axis in north China, most household incomes remain those of an emerging economy, not those of a developed one. The net effect of all this fragmentation may be positive for companies seeking consumers: people recognize the benefits enjoyed by their wealthier neighbors, and want to join their ranks.

The liberalization of China's markets has engendered ferocious competition. With companies continuing to take features and functions from their rivals as fast as they can, a single product's advantage may be very short-lived. Piracy and counterfeiting remain major problems, but increasingly companies are also finding themselves having to cope with streams of perfectly legitimate updates and upgrades. One of the reasons why Xiaomi iterates its products week by week is because it has to keep up with Lenovo, which offers 40 new smartphone models annually, and Huawei, which maintains a similar pace of launches.

These changes in China's openness over the last several years overall tend to benefit domestic private companies over both their multinational and state-owned rivals, largely because local companies have far greater familiarity with local conditions. Indeed, for many products, domestic competition is rising. Haier's strength in white goods is matched by firms such as TCL, Konka, and Changhong in televisions, Hangzhou Wahaha in beverages, and Lifan, Loncin, Zongshen, Jialing, and Qingqi in motorcycles—all names largely unknown outside China, but accounting for the majority of the goods in their respective categories.

Foreign companies are no longer needed to play the enabling role that Chinese businesses sought from them in the 1990s and 2000s. Chinese companies may not have all the access they would like to capital, technology, and know-how, but they are no longer starved of these things as they were 20 years ago. And when it comes to coping with the complexities of China's markets and business environment, they are usually far better placed to come up with answers then even the most experienced of multinationals.

For sure, some already-established foreign brands will continue to thrive, and new ones will join them. There are also some industries where Chinese companies have not yet made headway, even in their own country. The auto industry, for example, remains dominated by the big international companies via the joint ventures they operate with Chinese state-owned partners. Even the most successful of the local companies—Geely Auto, BYD, and Great Wall, all privately run—can only claim to have established a foothold so far. Luxury goods and other premium products, by and large, also remain the preserve of foreign brands.

That said, across most industries, Chinese companies have established themselves as serious rivals to multinationals. And increasingly, although China's markets are more open than ever before to foreign business, the nature of the business environment, in particular its complexity and speed of change, offer much advantage to indigenous companies. Externally based companies will be increasingly vulnerable to attacks from Chinese upstarts—as Xiaomi has shown, thanks to its access to the same contract manufacturing facilities and sourcing networks used by global firms.

OFFICIAL CHINA

Where open China provides the opportunities for China's entrepreneurs, official China, through its policies and administration, structures the environment in which those opportunities are found. Playing the key role in determining the form of those policies and administration are two priorities—an economic one, ensuring China's continued development, and a political one, ensuring the continued rule of the Chinese Communist Party. In the minds of China's leaders, this pair is inextricably linked: economic development must be maintained to ensure continuing support for Communist Party rule, while Communist Party rule provides the national stability necessary for development to continue.

The biggest problem facing China's leaders today is that, after three decades of high-speed expansion, the economy has reached a size and level of development where its growth rate will inevitably slow. Further reforms are necessary to hold that rate above a politically unacceptable level, especially given the country's rapid accumulation of debt in the aftermath of the global financial crisis, when the government spent heavily to support growth.

Much of that money was well spent on investments in roads, railways, and airports. Official China has also invested extensively in financial infrastructure. After Alipay opened up e-commerce, China UnionPay, a bank card network principally owned by China's four big state-owned banks, began installing point-of-sale terminals in every retail outlet of any size in the country. Financing companies were established, ensuring that people would have easy access to ways of buying big-ticket items such as cars or furniture with installment payments. The expansion of e-commerce companies also paved the way for improvements in the country's logistics. Its transportation and distribution industries have started to consolidate and invest in information systems, warehouse centers, and fleets of modern trucks.

Despite all this progress, major inefficiencies remain. Distribution, for example, continues to be a major headache for many companies, especially foreign ones. China's logistics costs, at 18 percent of GDP, remain stubbornly high—well above India's and double the level found in developed countries. Transporting goods from one part of the country to another usually involves multiple companies, each of them responsible for only part of the journey, many of them protected by local officials.

Since Xi Jinping assumed office in 2013, the government has proposed further economic liberalization. In his policy blueprint for the coming decade, announced in late 2013, Xi made it clear that China had to look beyond the state-driven investment that had sustained growth in recent years, and instead allow market forces to play a "decisive role" in the allocation of resources. Some of the measures he announced were aimed at improving the performance of state-owned enterprises, but the most important were those calling for a freer hand for the private sector, clearly identified as the country's principal source of innovation and growth.

Officials have already introduced various measures aimed at helping private companies, including making access to financing easier—such as the establishment of five independent banks specifically targeted at making loans to small- and medium-sized enterprises—streamlining procedures for setting up new companies, and encouraging the establishment of venture capital and private-equity funds.

Nonetheless, though China is allowing market forces a more important role, the goal of the government is not to create a free-market economy. Rather, it is to create an economy in which the market is a tool, not an end. The end is the creation of a powerful, modern China, in which the economy serves the state's needs.

To realize this goal, the Chinese government sees itself as playing a vital and continuing role. Through the 1990s and 2000s, it supported development by funding China's build-out of essential infrastructure. Today, urbanization has taken over as the key driver of growth. The state also has no intention of surrendering control over a range of key economic levers. Although the Chinese government plans ultimately to liberalize financial markets, for now it will continue to maintain capital controls that prevent money from flowing into or out of the country in destabilizing volumes, a managed exchange rate that allows it to support export industries, and officially set interest rates that give banks the cheap money they need to make policy loans. And, as I explore further in the next chapter, it will continue to pour enormous resources into scientific and technological research.

For now, official China's priority is maintaining stability. Like many of the country's external observers, it is worried about the possibility of a financial crisis. Unlike the majority of those observers, however, it is confident that it has the tools to ensure a crisis can be avoided. Almost all of China's debt is domestic, and most of it is held by state-owned banks, making it hard to see who could trigger a loss of confidence. Even if that were to happen, cash could always be made available to keep institutions solvent. Providing that the current rate of credit growth can be brought down, even at the slower rate of growth expected over the next decade, total debt will shrink relative to the size of the economy.

For private enterprises, Xi's policies overall are clearly good news, simultaneously increasing the resources available to them and leveling the playing field in markets where they compete with state-owned firms. The operational freedoms they have been granted over the last few decades will continue to be extended, and we will likely witness companies encroaching onto territory previously seen as the preserve of state-owned firms, such as finance and communications. Of course, the boundaries of what is acceptable still have to be negotiated, but whereas a few years ago it would have been all but certain that the interests of state-owned firms would prevail, now trusted private companies such as Alibaba or Tencent will be allowed far greater leeway.

In return, the government expects loyalty, particularly in politically sensitive areas. China's Internet businesses all hire staff to monitor their services, removing or blocking any anti-government messages. Few entrepreneurs object to this (at least not openly). As a body, they have little to gain from disturbing China's current political framework. For sure, many have changes they would like to see made, such as the clarification and strengthening of property rights, but almost all of them believe that such changes can be realized, over time, within the country's existing political framework.

While, as I noted in the previous chapter, many of China's entrepreneurs see themselves as bearers of wider responsibilities beyond business, this does not include questioning China's political framework, at least not in public. Indeed, the increasing visibility of entrepreneurs in official bodies may suggest the opposite—that they believe the best way to secure the changes they do want is to work within the system. Some entrepreneurs have started appearing with increasing frequency at official events, as part of the business delegations accompanying overseas tours by Chinese leaders, and more and more as delegates to official bodies. Tencent's Pony Ma and Xiaomi's Lei Jun are members of the country's parliament, the National People's Congress, and Baidu's Robin Li is a member of the Chinese People's Political Consultative Conference, the country's leading political advisory body.

In short, while official China is not ideologically committed to the rise of an entrepreneurial China, for pragmatic reasons it is hugely supportive. For entrepreneurs, this means they will be able to continue taking advantage of the opportunities created by open China without fear of them being taken away.

ONLINE CHINA

The final force driving opportunities for growth is technology, and particularly, as far as China's entrepreneurs are concerned, the Internet and its unique ability to transform the way industries and markets operate.

Overseas, much is made of official China's ability to monitor and control the Internet via its Great Firewall of China content management system. Within China, however, most people focus their attention on what the Internet offers as a source of growth, leading products and raising productivity. Indeed, many Chinese people hope that its often disruptive impact may at some point provide the means to allow China to catch up with or surpass the world's developed economies.

Since the mid 1990s, the government has invested heavily in rolling out and upgrading Internet infrastructure. Its current goals include high-speed broadband access in two-thirds of all homes by 2015, up from 40 percent in 2013, and raising mobile broadband penetration from 17 per 100 people to just under 1 in 3 over the same period.

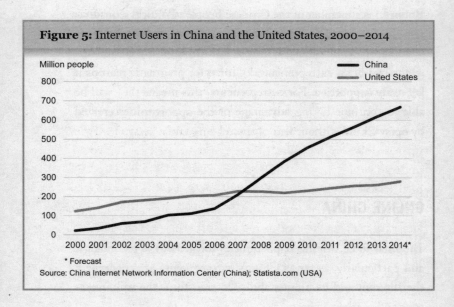

Figure 5: Internet Users in China and the United States, 2000–2014

Million people

China
United States

* Forecast

Source: China Internet Network Information Center (China); Statista.com (USA)

China's Disruptors

China's Internet user base overtook the United States's in 2007, and has continued to rise sharply ever since (see chart). With hundreds of millions of people in the countryside still unable to get online, that total looks set to keep rising by around 50 million a year at least into the early years of the next decade before flattening out. The country's mobile Internet users are increasing at an even greater rate, already numbering more than 500 million.

Though the government has kept the network backbone under total state control, private enterprises have from the start been free to rent bandwidth and establish almost any type of online business. As a result, e-commerce is one of the country's most open sectors, which in turn has led to the spectacular rise of China's Internet companies, above all the BAT trio: Baidu, Alibaba, and Tencent. These three have proved able to tap the SOOT formula better than any other businesses. They are beneficiaries of having the right technological capabilities to access the scale of China's population in a sector wide open to entry. In doing so, they take full advantage of the infrastructure built by official China and the assistance it has given in hindering access by companies such as Google and Facebook.

For the foreseeable future, propelled by the growth of e-commerce, the opportunities created by online technology will increase in size and number. But the structure of the sector could undergo major change. Until recently, each of the BATs occupied its own demarcated space, Baidu in search, Alibaba in e-commerce, and Tencent in online games and messaging. The arrival of the mobile Internet has upset this balance. With more people now accessing the Internet from their phones than from desktop computers, both Alibaba's dominance of e-commerce and Baidu's of search look vulnerable to Tencent, thanks to the near-universal presence of its WeChat messaging app on people's phones and the possibilities this offers the company to link directly to its own e-commerce and other services.

Moreover, a host of hungry Internet players are carving out their own empires, getting ready to compete with the BAT trio. These include Youku Tudou in online video; Vipshop, China's leading discount retailer; JD.com, the country's second-largest e-commerce business by volume of orders; and perhaps most aggressively, Beijing-based Qihoo 360, its main provider of Internet security software. Founded by Zhou Hongyi in 2005, its free Internet security software first became ubiquitous on Chinese computers (where it has at least 450 million users) and now on smartphones (with a claimed 640 million users). Along the way, Zhou has launched a series of related ventures, some successful, others not. After adding a browser to his company's offerings, he decided to go head-to-head with Baidu in search, clawing his way to a market share of nearly 20 percent. Next, he entered the smartphone market via a succession of partnerships with handset makers Huawei, TCL, Haier, and Alcatel. Though sales were poor, the publicity they generated for Qihoo's security software more than compensated. Most recently, Zhou successfully took on the mobile app market, claiming first position in China's crowded market with its store, 360 Mobile Assistant.

PONYING UP

During the next few years, it is likely that one or more of China's other Internet firms will rise to rival the members of the BAT trio. So far, outside China, Alibaba has gotten the lion's share of attention because of its highly publicized initial public offering in September 2014, which raised $25 billion. Tencent, though less well known outside of China, is decidedly the bigger company, with both greater revenues—$9.9 billion in 2013 to Alibaba's $7.5 billion—and greater profits—$3.15 billion over Alibaba's $2.85 billion. And until Jack Ma took his company public in the United States, Tencent's CEO, Pony Ma, was comfortably the richer of the two.

Though not related, the two Mas share both a surname and a take-no-prisoners attitude to business. Pony Ma, however, has the greater reputation for fierce competitiveness. He once went so far as to claim that "[To] copy is not evil," and he is well known for using Tencent's financial muscle to streamroller smaller companies into selling or sharing him their software. That's why Tencent has grown so rapidly; every company in China has benefited from the SOOT factors, but Tencent has also benefited from a shrewd, resolute approach to making the most of those factors.

Born in 1971 in south China's Guangdong Province, Ma studied computer science at Shenzhen University, then worked briefly for a paging company before setting up Tencent in 1998 with a friend, Zhang Zhidong, who served as the company's chief technology officer until stepping down for personal reasons in September 2014. Within a year, the pair had developed their first popular product, a free instant-messaging program for computers called QQ, a copy of an Israeli program called ICQ. The program soon attracted enough users to persuade U.S. investment firm IDG and Richard Li, the son of Hong Kong tycoon Li Ka-shing, to buy stakes in the company. Briefly the company looked like it might be a hit, but as the months passed and revenues failed to materialize, IDG and Li sold their stakes to a South African media company, Naspers, which for $32 million acquired a 47 percent stake.

Tencent entered the 2000s desperately short of funds, barely able to keep its servers running. Casting around for sources of even the smallest cash flow to tide them over, Ma and his team launched a handful of lost-cost add-on services, each priced at just a few cents a month. Unexpectedly, one of them, an application that allowed mobile phone users to send QQ messages to computers, proved hugely popular. Almost by chance, Tencent had stumbled over its business model: selling value-adding extras to users of a product given away for nothing.

Of course, that free product had to be popular to get the scale needed for its success. But as QQ became China's primary means of personal communication, used on both computers and mobile phones, popularity ceased to be an issue. Pony Ma did not rest, however. In rapid succession, Tencent added features and services, knowing that, with a user base that even today still has an astonishing 800 million active accounts, even the tiniest response rates would generate a sizable stream of revenue.

By 2004, Tencent was doing well enough to list on the Hong Kong Stock Exchange. The company used some of the $200 million it raised to launch a handful of online games. Distributed for free via its QQ user base, the games were a hit—and they revealed a whole new market for virtual goods, far greater than the market for its QQ add-on services. Through the remainder of the decade, Tencent devoted itself to becoming the main force in Chinese online games, buying up popular games from around the world, adapting them for the Chinese market, then cashing in on sales of virtual extras.

The company has since gone on to add a host of other services, from search and social media to music and video streaming. So far, none has come close to rivaling its games as a source of revenue. In 2013, sales of games-related virtual goods earned the company $4 billion of its total revenues; another $4 billion came from other added-value services, and less than $1 billion from other sources, including e-commerce and advertising. By not relying on advertising as its main source of revenue, Tencent distinguishes itself not just from its two Chinese peers, Alibaba and Baidu, but from the giants of the U.S. Internet sector: Facebook, Google, and Twitter. Of course, it still has to come up with a continual stream of ideas for services that it can persuade people to pay for, but having a user base of hundreds of millions of people for each of its core free services—instant messaging, games, and WeChat—gives Tencent an enormous advantage.

Tencent's reliance on business generated via a free application will likely continue through at least one more cycle thanks to its latest hit, the smartphone messaging app WeChat. Launched at the start of 2011, WeChat's growth has been nothing short of phenomenal, reaching nearly 470 million users by late 2014.

The service is already acting as a gateway pushing users toward mobile games and other paid-for services. And if it can give Tencent an opening into mobile e-commerce, it could in time prove to be the company's most important giveaway, allowing it to take on Alibaba in one of the latter's few areas of weakness, its lack of a mobile presence.

Through late 2013 and 2014, both Tencent and Alibaba went on acquisition sprees, with much of their spending—Tencent's purchase of a stake in JD.com, China's second-biggest online retailer after Tmall, for example, or Alibaba's nearly $600 million purchase of a chunk of Sina Weibo, China's biggest microblogging Web site—clearly aimed at countering one another. Though Tencent's online payments system, Tenpay, badly lags Alipay in terms of popularity, the addition of electronic payment capability to WeChat in 2013, bolstered by a vigorous campaign to attract users—including a highly popular Red Packet application that allowed people to swap gifts of money via their phones at Chinese New Year—could change things.

But perhaps the biggest sign of an upcoming struggle was the formation of an $815 million joint venture between China's second-, third-, and fourth-richest figures—Pony Ma, Baidu's Robin Li, and Wang Jianlin, the chairman of Dalian Wanda. Named Wanda E-Commerce, its explicit target is Alibaba's e-commerce empire.

According to Wanda's Wang, the venture's aim is to build a seamless online-to-offline shopping experience that draws on his company's nationwide network of commercial properties, Tencent's online social networks and electronic payment systems, and Baidu's search and big-data capabilities.

ALWAYS ON THE EDGE

Loosening Alibaba's grip on China's e-commerce sector will not be easy. What could make it possible are the features of China's business environment explored in this chapter: opportunities arising from China's scale and rate of growth, the ferocious competition of its open markets, technology's impact on its landscape, or, possibly, a change in outlook from official China. Indeed, the challenges faced by these entrepreneurs are prevalent in every industry, and companies must constantly be on the watch for unexpected disruptions.

Competition will be the biggest threat for most businesses. In e-commerce, the market scale and growth rates that created Alibaba are also allowing a host of other businesses to grow at breakneck rates. JD.com, an online seller of electronic goods, went public on the Nasdaq Stock Exchange in May 2014 on the back of revenues rising more than a third faster than Alibaba's. It quickly saw its valuation rise to $40 billion. Hot on its heels is a company I look at in detail in the next chapter, Yihaodian, an online supermarket that rose to become one of only five Chinese e-commerce companies with annual revenues of more than 10 billion yuan within five years of its establishment.

Competition is particularly fierce in the mobile phone industry. Xiaomi is not the only Chinese smartphone maker looking to pressure Apple and Samsung. Both Lenovo and Huawei have targeted global markets for their handset divisions. Neither has the same marketing savvy as Xiaomi, especially in reaching out to younger customers. But with far stronger R&D resources, financial muscle, and distribution networks, via telecom operators in Huawei's case and through retail networks in Lenovo's, they will pounce if Xiaomi stumbles.

Official China could ultimately pick sides in these competitions, and thereby greatly increase the fortunes of the favored. To bypass rules banning foreign investment in China's Internet, every one of China's Internet companies which has listed overseas—including Alibaba, Tencent, and Baidu—has done so through a legal structure known as a variable-interest entity. These are companies, registered in offshore financial centers such as the Cayman Islands, with contracts to receive the profits of the Chinese companies, not ownership of their actual China-based assets.

So far, despite existing in a regulatory gray area, these vehicles have withstood legal scrutiny. That could change, especially if the government decided it wanted to exercise greater control over a sector that has long had the habit of operating in areas beyond official oversight. As Alibaba noted in its IPO filing documents: "It is uncertain whether any new [Chinese] laws, rules or regulations relating to variable-interest entity structures will be adopted, or if adopted, what they would provide." Most likely, however, is that officials will continue to tolerate the current status quo, happy to see businesses such as Alibaba and Tencent benefit by raising funds or extending their operations into foreign markets, but knowing they can always rein them in with administrative measures if necessary.

The challenge China's business environment poses for its entrepreneurs is how to organize their companies to cope with this environment—to have the vision to see opportunities, the capabilities to seize and develop them, the toughness and resources to see off competition, and the political skills to stay onside with officials. How companies develop and deploy these abilities is the subject of my next chapter.

3

DO OR DIE

Outsiders who get information about China from the Western media tend to view it as an innovation desert: a country of copycat firms, weak or nonexistent intellectual-property rights, and an education system based on rote learning.

Addressing a group of air force cadets in May 2014, U.S. vice president Joe Biden declared, "I challenge you, name me one innovative project, one innovative change, one innovative product that has come out of China." Two months earlier, *Harvard Business Review* published an article with the headline "Why China Can't Innovate." The piece, written by business-school professors Regina M. Abrami, William C. Kirby, and F. Warren McFarlan, boldly declared: "Today, . . . many believe that the West is home to creative business thinkers and innovators, and that China is largely a land of rule-bound rote learners—a place where R&D is diligently pursued but breakthroughs are rare."

The authors agreed with this outlook and dismissed the kind of advances seen at companies such as Alibaba and Baidu as "second-generation" innovation—adaptations of existing technologies for the Chinese market, and the kind of routine work companies around the world do day in and day out once someone else has done the blue-sky thinking.

This is bizarre. How can the authors of this article and many other similar pieces miss the impact that companies in a wide range of industries are having in China, reworking daily life by inventing and applying new ideas in a variety of fields? Consider Haier in white goods. Huawei in telecommunications. Xiaomi in mobile phones. Alibaba in e-commerce and finance. Tencent in messaging and gaming. These are just a few examples; there are many more. Yet they are often overlooked. Why?

The simplest explanation is a gap in expectations. Chinese companies have yet to produce basic technological research in power systems or chemicals, for example, or a product or service that has had the same impact on Western markets as the iPhone or Facebook, or a praised and adopted business process such as Japan's "just-in-time" production system. But translating this into "China isn't innovative" misses the point entirely. Focusing on what has not happened in China means not seeing what is actually taking place.

ONLY THE INNOVATIVE GROW

"For entrepreneurial companies, innovation is do or die," says Yihaodian's chairman Yu Gang. He reels off a list of initiatives his company, China's biggest online supermarket, has launched to drive and manage growth. It has turned subway stations into virtual stores where people shop with their smartphones by snapping bar codes that appear alongside pictures of products. It is automatically tracking prices for several million goods across 72 competitors' Web sites. It has installed innovative cross-company inventory-tracking systems with its partners. It has streamlined pallet handling at distribution centers.

None of these were groundbreaking, he willingly concedes, but every one had played a role in driving Yihaodian's customer total from 1 million in 2009 to 60 million in 2013. Its revenues of $1.8 billion that year made it one of China's top five e-commerce businesses. Selling everyday items, priced marginally lower than those offered in brick-and-mortar stores, and delivering them through the congested streets of China's cities directly to customers' homes or offices on fleets of motorcycles and mopeds has proved a hit.

To reach this point, Yu took a roundabout journey. Born in Yichang, a city on the Yangtze in central China, after graduating from Wuhan University in 1983 he moved to the United States, where he became a business-school professor at the University of Texas. Yu went on to launch an airlines-related computer systems business that he eventually sold to Andersen Consulting (the forerunner of Accenture) and worked as a multinational executive running Amazon's and Dell's global supply chains. His job at Dell took him back to China, with a post in Shanghai managing the company's $18 billion procurement budget.

For most people, that would have been challenge enough. But Yu found himself caught up in the tide of entrepreneurial fever that was sweeping the country. The idea for Yihaodian emerged from a business lunch with fellow Dell executive—and current Yihaodian CEO—Liu Junling. Both men were intrigued by the possibility of creating a business able to cope with the logistical complexities of meeting the everyday needs of China's rising urban class.

In 2012, Wal-Mart Stores bought 50.2 percent of the company, granting Yihaodian access to Wal-Mart's network of warehouses across China and further logistics know-how. With Yihaodian still operating in the red as of late 2014, Yu's goal is to accelerate its customer growth continuously and to double its revenues by 2015. That means expanding on every front: finding tens of millions of new customers each year, handling their data, monitoring and tracking the ever-rising number and volume of goods moving in and out of its distribution centers, and keeping pace with the technological developments of its competitors.

Yihaodian's trajectory echoes that of China's fast-changing cities. With rapid growth, dense populations, and increasingly long commutes, time and convenience are at a premium. A rising volume of mobile commerce has seen sales increase in the evenings and on weekends. With incomes rising, more people want fresh produce, while concerns about food safety have made imported foods one of Yihaodian's fastest-growing categories.

As of 2013, e-commerce accounted for 8 percent of China's retail sales. Yet retailers are already seeing shrinking sales at many supermarkets and other brick-and-mortar stores. So far, cities in China's eastern coastal provinces account for the biggest volume of online purchases, though growth is rising fastest in inland provinces, where incomes are lower but a lack of brick-

and-mortar alternatives means that online shopping is many people's first choice.

If Yihaodian can sustain its growth, it has the potential to reshape China's retail landscape. But only a management style that ensures constant improvement and ongoing innovation will make it possible for the business to remain relevant. The imperative that Yihaodian and other leading entrepreneurial companies face, therefore, is to come up with a continuous flow of ideas and approaches that foster and support rapid growth. The imperatives of China's business environment—scale, open markets, official support, and technology, as described in the last chapter—are driving this innovation. The growth in China requires companies to change, not as a reaction to one particular problem, but as an across-the-board need to cope with multiple challenges simultaneously. A typical manufacturer, for example, might find itself facing the following challenges:

★ **Continuously updating its products.** As long as intellectual-property protection remains weak, companies know that any change or improvement in their products will be immediately copied by a rival. To stay ahead, they must generate a continual flow of new features and functions to keep their customers happy and make it harder for competitors to keep up with them.

★ **Controlling costs.** With most consumers in China still highly price-sensitive, offering goods at a lower cost per unit remains a key goal for almost every company. Building scale is part of the answer, along with trimming production costs, reducing material inputs, and developing goods with only the functions or features their buyers need.

★ **Managing talent shortages.** Shortages of skilled and experienced staff have long been a problem for Chinese companies, exacerbated by the country's growth rate. In many key areas, businesses cope through adopting guerrilla strategies as a way of coping. Take marketing, where a lack of experience at running traditional promotional campaigns forces companies to develop their own offbeat ways of attracting and retaining new customers. An example of this is Xiaomi's use of crowdsourcing to get input on ways of improving its phones and to create a buzz for each new release.

★ **Coping with wage pressures.** Companies also need to innovate to overcome China's shrinking labor force and fast-rising costs. Fifteen years ago, Chinese workers were among the cheapest in the world, with average monthly wages of less than $100, one-third the rate of Mexico's. By 2013, that average had risen to $700, on a par with Malaysia's, and more than one-third higher than Mexico's. Making matters harder, the country's workforce is shrinking. Through the rest of this decade, the decline will be modest, with China's working population falling by between 2 and 4 million people annually—barely noticeable in a total working-age population of 900 million. But after 2020, thanks to the country's one-child family policy introduced in the late 1970s, the numbers will fall precipitously as the workforce falls to 650 million by mid-century. Productivity will have to rise sharply if China is to stay competitive. Rising standards of education, discussed later in this chapter, will help, but so will new ways of organizing workforces, such as the platform-based system that Zhang Ruimin is experimenting with at Haier.

★ **Overcoming infrastructure shortcomings.** China's road and rail build-out has been impressive. But with more than 90 percent of the country's 65,000 miles of expressway and all of its 7,000 miles of high-speed rail having been built in the last 15 years, many lower-tier cities and towns have had little time or opportunity to develop modern retail outlets such as malls.

Companies in other industries face similar lists of pressures. To address them, a company must be continually inventive across the entire range of its functions and operations. Coming up with answers cannot be something that is handled by its research arm, made part of its strategic plan, or treated as a process aimed at creating long-term sustainable advantages. It has to be part of the everyday operations of all of its parts. Rita Gunther McGrath, a professor at Columbia Business School, has aptly described the necessary process as "exploiting temporary competitive advantages."

Fortunately, this pressure also has a counterweight: balancing the stresses of China's market openness are its opportunities for entrepreneurship. Alibaba's creation of Alipay is an apt example. At one level, it was a response forced on the company because of China's lack of an online payments system, but on another, far more important one, it opened the way for the establishment of e-commerce in China. The creation of Alipay was not an isolated development. More often than not, each improvement a Chinese company makes, whether incremental or calling for a bold leap into a new business area, is just one of multiple reactions a company has to come up with to cope with the circumstances in which it operates. The cumulative effect of this need to always be coming up with answers to operating problems is what makes Chinese innovation so powerful.

The greatest opportunities for entrepreneurship occur where the Internet is pulling down barriers between industries, though this does not mean the challenge is restricted to technology. A company such as Yihaodian is developing not just the technology and online systems needed for an e-commerce business, but an overarching business model. In this case, Yihaodian has to determine whether it can fulfill its comprehensive transportation needs in a variety of Chinese cities with a system of motorcycles and mopeds. If it can, it could end up owning the deliveries of food and other everyday necessities across China. If it can't, then likely it will fall by the wayside.

If it fails, then almost certainly another company will replace it. SF Express, for example, is China's biggest privately owned express delivery company. In 2014, it began rolling out a chain of 400 brick-and-mortar convenience stores equipped with computer terminals to test whether it could successfully add e-commerce to its logistics expertise. If the company can't compete effectively with Yihaodian, then the replacement might possibly be a collection of companies. Alibaba is trying to arrange that kind of consortium through a string of deals. One, with China Post, aims to deliver online purchases anywhere in the country within 24 hours. Another, with Haier, aims to facilitate the delivery of large goods. There is also the founding of a technology consortium with several courier firms, and a $250 million investment in Singapore's national post service, SingPost. Yu's comment that "innovation is do or die" underlines just how critical it is for businesses to be innovating in continuous waves, and China's rate of development has made it a breeding ground for such agile corporate players in all areas. As we have seen, the natural state for Haier and Xiaomi, as well as at Tencent and Alibaba, is one of continual across-the-board change. This is a market where only the fittest survive.

Innovation, in this case, means process and practice innovation as well as product and service innovation. Twenty years ago, it was rare to find an ethic of continuous improvement in Chinese companies. Now it is pervasive. Indeed, it has become a prerequisite for business expansion—either into new industries and service categories or outside China to the world at large.

A GLOBAL MODEL?

While most of these improvements have made companies stronger within China, they are also beginning to have an effect elsewhere. The common thread running through the growth of all these companies is continual, incremental innovation in every area of their operations as a response to China's business environment. But some of these companies are also discovering they can use a similar approach to grow globally. One company that has done this with enormous effect is Shenzhen-based Huawei Technologies. In a quarter of a century Huawei has made itself the world's biggest manufacturer of telecom-network equipment, rivaled only by Sweden's Ericsson.

Huawei's founder, Ren Zhengfei, was born in 1944 in southwest China's Guizhou Province, one of the country's poorest regions. Ren attended university, studying engineering, and then joined the People's Liberation Army to work on military-related technologies. He left the army in the early 1980s as part of a round of military downsizing, moving to Shenzhen to start his own business. After a few false starts, he used 21,000 yuan of his own savings (then worth about $5,600) to set up Huawei in 1987.

Initially, Huawei's main source of revenue came from selling office telecom equipment imported from Hong Kong. By 1990, it had acquired enough resources to open its first research laboratory. Two years later, the company launched its first digital switch, the core piece of equipment at the heart of any telecom network, which directs signals to and from callers.

China at that time had just embarked on a massive telecom rollout; within less than 10 years, the country went from having no private telephones to acquiring first a nationwide fixed-line network and then multiple mobile ones. The big winners for most of this period were the international equipment makers—Siemens, Alcatel, Nokia, Motorola, Ericsson, and Nortel—all of whom found ready customers in the provincial arms of the country's big telecom services providers: China Telecom, China Mobile, and China Unicom.

These companies' best Chinese customers were in the richer provinces and cities of the east coast, from Guangdong in the south to Beijing and Tianjin in the north, where buyers preferred to get their hands on the more advanced equipment offered by the international vendors. But a government rule saying that all provinces had to buy equipment from at least two suppliers opened the door for Huawei to become the second provider in poorer, inland regions. Orders were small at first, which allowed Huawei's engineers to gain experience at both installing equipment and seeing how what they made measured up against the systems from the international suppliers.

Driven by Ren's insistence that Huawei continually upgrade its products' quality through research and development, and supported by a government eager to see indigenous equipment makers displace foreign companies, the company's footprint grew. The performance of its switches still lagged that of its competitors, but cheaper prices compensated for the gap. Able to undercut foreign companies on price and out-compete Chinese state-owned companies on quality, Ren began to find buyers in richer coastal provinces.

In 1997, Huawei stretched across the border immediately to Shenzhen's south to secure its first international deal, a contract with Hong Kong operator Hutchison Telecom. Within eight years, as it extended sales first across Asia, then Africa and Latin America, and finally into Europe, Huawei's overseas revenues were greater than its domestic ones. To ensure it secured deals, Ren insisted that his sales staff always submit bids below those of competitors—typically, by 5 to 15 percent, according to a report by Wharton Business School. From the start, there was also another side to Huawei's business: regardless of a customer's size, the company would always be willing to come in and look for ways of improving the operations of its clients. During the golden era of telecom growth through the 1990s until the dot-com collapse, this approach was very different from that of the big international vendors, whose main focus was developing cutting-edge technology which they could then sell to fast-growing telecom operators. Their preference was for selling entire systems to big companies, and they had little interest in selling to smaller businesses, especially those in poorer markets.

Huawei, in contrast, was happy to work with such customers, focusing on their often prosaic needs. It developed smaller, more power-efficient mobile base stations that allowed operators to reduce their electricity and rental bills. The company honed its ability to integrate its equipment with existing systems. And, perhaps most important, it rapidly expanded the number of its R&D staff, hiring thousands of computer programmers and software-engineering graduates fresh from university, and putting them to work figuring out ways in which operators could run their networks more efficiently.

Today, Huawei is China's biggest private exporter, with two-thirds of its $39 billion in revenues coming from overseas. It sells to markets in almost every part of the world, with the glaring exception of the United States, where its sales have been restricted to a handful of small mobile operators, largely due to national security concerns in Washington. Unsubstantiated allegations that the company is an agent of the Chinese government, however, serve as a smoke screen to hide Huawei's significance. It has shown how innovation, instead of calling for a string of ground-breaking products, can also be about finding ways of supplying and supporting an appropriate version of a product to secondary-market players. Serving customers in China's lower-tier regions and other less-developed countries, then working with smaller players in developed markets, allowed Huawei to gain footholds and experience without having to go head-to-head with the big European and American equipment makers. Instead, accompanied by a constant push to narrow the technological gap on its rivals, it could focus on growth through stealth by eroding their market share in areas they usually regarded as of secondary importance.

As it grew in scale, Huawei's consistently cheaper prices also had the effect of commoditizing the telecom-equipment sector, in the process reducing its competitors' profits. While its rivals could still win contracts where technological prowess mattered, less frequently could they win them where operators simply wanted their networks extended or upgraded in a routine manner.

Along the way, Huawei has gradually transformed the world's telecom-equipment market into something resembling China, where what counted was being able to offer constant incremental improvements in technology, features tailored to meet the precise needs of cost-conscious operators with no extra frills, and always at a price a little better than anyone else's. Year by year, other companies merged or exited the industry, as Huawei relentlessly forced margins downward. By 2012, it had established itself as the world's biggest network-infrastructure vendor, with Ericsson its only remaining serious rival, and second only to Cisco in the router and switching market.

THE STATE STEPS UP

In Chapter 4, I look further at the threats Chinese entrepreneurial companies pose to businesses around the world as more and more of them take their domestically honed practices overseas. Now, however, I want to turn and look at the force that will be responsible for adding an entirely new dimension to the innovative repertoire of Chinese companies.

To date, because of their market-driven nature, the innovations of most Chinese companies remain limited by the fact that, while they allow companies to grow and extend themselves, their focus is inherently short term.

What will change the capacity of Chinese companies to innovate on a far greater and more ambitious scale are measures being undertaken by official China. The government has long known that for China to achieve its goal of becoming a developed economy, the country must be an innovation power. Despite the commonly held belief of many Western observers that only companies can innovate, China's leaders are aware that companies alone cannot make the massive long-term commitment of resources needed to drive innovation in many crucial areas, so the state has to lead the way.

Their inspiration is America's current technological supremacy, and its origins in the U.S. government's huge R&D investments of the 1950s and '60s that underpin much of today's computing, communications, energy, and other advanced technologies. To become a similar power, official China knows it too must spend heavily on industrial and scientific research and development and fund a massive expansion of education, especially in science and engineering.

Though the government started upping its spending on R&D in the mid 1990s, the turning point was the launching, in 2006, of an ambitious 15-year plan to raise R&D expenditure to 2.5 percent of GDP, with energy, water resources, and environmental protection identified as top research priorities. This move catapulted China up the list of national R&D spenders. While the United States remains by far the world's largest investor in R&D, accounting for about one-third of the global total, China has risen to second place, with its total—now well past $200 billion annually—accounting for nearly 15 percent of the world total, and more than four times bigger than its spending in the early 2000s (see chart).

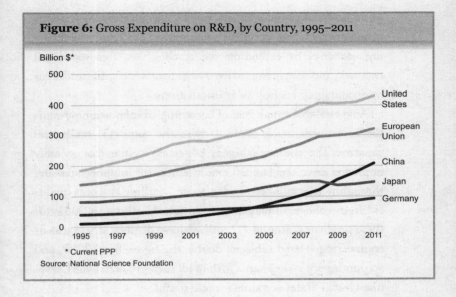

Figure 6: Gross Expenditure on R&D, by Country, 1995–2011

Billion $*

* Current PPP
Source: National Science Foundation

Its R&D intensity (R&D spending expressed as a percentage of GDP) has also jumped from around half a percent in the 1990s to 2 percent now, just above that of the EU, though behind the United States (2.8 percent) and Japan (3.4 percent).

So far, much of China's official spending has been aimed at matching Western capabilities and achievements, not at pushing forward into new areas. The rationale is straightforward: unless Chinese scientists and engineers can do the same things as their Western counterparts, they will not be able to move beyond their achievements. Again, the suggestions that China's corporate innovation amounts to nothing beyond playing catch-up is to miss the across-the-board scale of what is happening, and that its impact is principally aimed at enabling China to cope with the immediate challenges it faces, such as reducing its reliance on imported technologies via developing an indigenous semi-conductor industry, strengthening its trade links with neighboring countries by extending the reach of its high-speed rail network, and simply improving access to electricity in rural areas by encouraging rooftop solar installations.

Also vital to China's goal of becoming an innovation power is the investment being made to raise the country's intellectual capacity. The country's higher education system has steadily improved over the last 20 years, while the numbers passing through it have climbed. Today, some 7 million students graduate from college annually, up from just 1 million in 2001. Of these graduates, around 1.2 million have degrees in science- or engineering-related subjects, double the figure from 2000, and accounting for more than a fifth of all such graduates worldwide (the United States accounts for one-tenth).

At the higher end, of 200,000 doctorates in science and engineering awarded around the world in 2010, some 33,000 were from U.S. universities, with China just behind with 31,000 (in third place was Russia with 16,000, then Germany with 12,000, and the United Kingdom with 11,000). Chinese students also account for around one-quarter of all foreign students obtaining doctorates in science and engineering from U.S. universities.

At China's colleges and universities, students, connected to the world via their computers and smartphones, often fluent in English, are as informed and sophisticated as their counterparts in any other part of the world. By 2020, they will form part of a total graduate workforce numbering nearly 200 million—more than the entire U.S. workforce.

THE PACE OF INNOVATION

How quickly could China's investment in education and innovation lead to breakthrough results or business success? In some areas, it already has. The quality of China's traded goods, for example, is rising rapidly. In 2009, low-value goods such as toys and plastic products accounted for 40 percent of China's exports. Now they account for less than one-third, largely due to increasing overseas sales of industrial machinery, automotive components, and other higher-value goods.

Agriculture has also seen substantial improvements. Over the past 20 years China has increased its grain productivity by 2.6 percent annually, sufficient to raise output by two-thirds per unit of land. Yields could rise even further thanks to a new strain of rice (developed jointly by the Bill and Melinda Gates Foundation, the Chinese Academy of Agriculture Sciences, and a Chinese biotechnology institute) that has already been found to increase output by 20 percent in test projects.

State-funded medical research is starting to spill over to private companies. In 2009, Nasdaq-listed Sinovac Biotech developed the first effective vaccine for swine flu in just 87 days. Before then, almost all new rapid vaccine developments had been completed by American or European research teams. Headquartered in Beijing, Sinovac Biotech is currently awaiting approval for a vaccine against the EV71 virus that causes hand, foot, and mouth disease in children and is conducting clinical trials for a vaccine that could protect people from one of the most common bacterial causes of pneumonia and meningitis.

In manufacturing, China is starting to benefit from advances in digital technology. The last few years have seen much speculation on the possibility of robots and 3D printing leading to a "reshor-ing" of manufacturing back to developed countries, including the United States. The likelihood, however, is rather the oppo-site: as Chinese companies refine their ability to introduce new practices and technologies to enhance their manufacturing prow-ess, they will find themselves in a strong position to claim a greater share of higher-end processes.

Robots are widely regarded as a solution to worker shortages and rising wages. After robotics sales to China rose 25 percent annually from 2005 to 2012, and then jumped 36 percent in 2013, China is now the world's biggest industrial robot market, accounting for one-fifth of all sales. Many of these robots are used in the auto industry, where the number deployed rose from just over 50 per 10,000 staff in 2006 to more than 200 as of mid 2014. In Zhejiang, one of China's leading industrial provinces, just to the south of Shanghai, officials have committed $82 bil-lion over the five years through 2017 for factories to invest in automating production lines.

China is making big steps to realize its goal of being the world's leading developer of 3D printing technology. It already produces machines that can make steel and other heavy metal components up to six meters (nearly 20 feet) in diameter and weighing up to 300 tons for use in nuclear, thermal, hydro-, and other power applications. Perhaps its most impressive develop-ment to date is a printer that builds titanium alloy structures, including the landing gear, main force-bearing frames, and wind-shield frames for a narrow-body airliner being developed by Commercial Aircraft Corporation of China as a rival to similar aircraft from Boeing and Airbus. Printing the main windshield frame of a C919 using 3D printing technology takes 55 days and costs less than $200,000. Traditional techniques would take around two years and cost $2 million.

Industry groups forecast that by 2016, the country's 3D printer market will be worth around $1.65 billion, 10 times bigger than in 2012, and large enough to displace the United States as the world's largest user of 3D printing technology. While most developments continue to take place within state-owned companies, private companies are also making strides in this arena. In June 2014, a Qingdao-based company unveiled a printer able to produce objects measuring up to 12 meters (about 40 feet) high, wide, and deep—large enough to fabricate a house. Using glass fiber–reinforced plastics, the printer can produce entire buildings in one run, giving it a role in areas such as post-earthquake reconstruction.

PRIVATE BACKING

As China becomes richer and develops more products of its own instead of adapting those from other places, more financial support for innovation will accompany its growth. Innovation will also become easier as start-ups and other small companies get greater access to the resources they need.

One company leading the way in developing the soft infrastrucure neccessary is Innovation Works, a technology incubator and venture capital firm founded by Taiwan-born Kai-fu Lee. Lee has long been one of China's most popular microbloggers, with more than 50 million people following his Sina Weibo postings.

Born in 1961, Lee moved to the United States with his family in the 1970s. After studying computing at Columbia University and earning a PhD from Carnegie Mellon University for research into speech recognition technology, he worked at some of the biggest names in American computing, including Apple, Silicon Graphics, and Microsoft, before moving to Beijing with Google. There he established Google China and built a huge following as a commentator on China-related technology and social issues.

In 2009, at almost the same time as Yihaodian's Yu Gang, he ended his multinational career to start Innovation Works. Using funds from several powerful backers, including YouTube cofounder Steve Chen, Taiwanese contract electronics manufacturer Foxconn, and Legend Holdings, the parent company of Lenovo, Lee has since backed more than 50 companies, helping them with legal and recruitment support, office space, and funding. Although Lee has yet to have a major hit, Innovation Works has played a key role in drawing attention to the huge number of Internet and technology start-ups being founded in China.

Other successful businesspeople are also reinvesting in young companies. Lei Jun, in addition to growing Xiaomi, set up a venture capital fund, Shunwei China, in 2011 with $200 million of funding. Foxconn has also started looking for new electronics start-ups for Innocon, its own manufacturing incubation center based in a former Nokia factory in Beijing's southeastern outskirts. Its goal is helping small technology manufacturers manage the transition to mass production in the hope of discovering the world's next consumer electronic hit.

Whereas a decade ago most funding came from technology multinationals, more is now coming from venture capital funds.

Foreign investors are coming too. Sequoia Capital's China arm, run by Neil Shen, one of the cofounders of Ctrip, China's leading online travel agency, leads the field with its investments, which include antivirus firm Qihoo 360 and discount retailer Vipshop. Most investments from abroad continue to be small, but their volume is increasing. In October 2014, for example, Intel Capital announced that its China Smart Device Innovation Fund had made its first investments, totaling $28 million, in several Chinese companies.

TOMORROW'S CHINA

With Chinese per capita GDP still only one-ninth of America's, most successful innovations are aimed at goods or services that appeal to tens or hundreds of millions of people, aiming to take a little bit of money from each of them, as is the goal of companies such as Tencent and Xiaomi. But as China grows richer, more innovations will be aimed at wealthier segments of the market, and so more of its innovations will also appeal to people in developed economies. As the American economist Alex Tabarrok has pointed out, "If China and India were as rich as the United States is today, the market for cancer drugs would be eight times larger than it is now."

Obviously this type of growth will be good for everyone, but it will be particularly good for Chinese innovators, who, with their knowledge of local conditions, will be best placed to take advantage of the opportunities in China to develop products they can then take to other markets worldwide.

As this happens, China will also strengthen its links with global innovation networks, especially on the Internet, leading to more cross-border collaboration. Indeed, one of the defining features of future innovation will be that, as findings and improvements made in one place can readily be adopted or used in another, we will see a world in which innovations—regardless of where they come from—will be shared and applied at an accelerating pace.

China's regulatory and legal infrastructure is also becoming both more innovation-friendly and more rigorous in monitoring the value and safety of the innovations. In medicine, for example, a number of major scandals undermined confidence in Chinese products in the 2000s, most prominently the more than 80 deaths in the United States caused by using a blood thinner using contaminated Chinese ingredients. Tighter government monitoring and heavier punishments for those found in breach of rules have improved matters significantly, with companies also spending a lot more to ensure their operations meet World Health Organization standards and, in some instances, submitting products to the WHO for approval.

Companies are also finally finding it easier to protect their intellectual property. In late 2013, a complaint from Youku Tudou, China's biggest online video provider, led to search engine Baidu being fined 250,000 yuan ($40,000) for copyright violations. The amount—the maximum allowable under Chinese law—was derisory compared with Baidu's 10.52 billion yuan ($1.74 billion) profits that year. But the search company, which in its early years had built a reputation as being a great tool for finding pirated music, has since been active in removing pirated material from its video Web site.

Ultimately, the biggest beneficiary of China's approach to innovation will be China itself. Urbanization is by far the biggest change China is undergoing. The society that will emerge from this process—several hundred cities, ranging in size from a million or so people to several tens of millions of people—will be like no other society the world has seen before.

If these cities are to be livable, China will have to find solutions in two crucial areas: energy and transport. Between them, this pair is repsonsible for the country's greatest environmental ills. Relying on coal for two-thirds of its energy needs has made China the world's biggest carbon emitter. Pollution from its coal-fueled power plants is responsible for more than a quarter of a million premature deaths and 140 million days of sick leave annually. Vehicles, thanks to the 120 million cars and trucks now on China's roads, have become the second-biggest source of pollution after coal, and have made the country the world's number-one oil importer.

China will need years, and probably decades, of change in these two areas, across multiple fronts. Progress will likely be slow. Yet it is here that the potential for China's approach to innovation can be discerned. The techniques called for—patient but relentless incremental improvements across the board, with the occasional leap into a new area—are the very same that Chinese companies are using to advance their businesses now. As Huawei has shown, the outcome can be a radical reworking of their industry.

Perhaps it is no coincidence that many of China's most creative entrepreneurs, who have built great businesses by constantly augmenting and refining their operations, adding scale, and then making bold leaps into new areas, are now approaching environmental issues with an eye toward contributing to change. When they look at the environment, they see a combination of an enormous problem that needs solving and a huge opportunity. In short, a challenge similar in structure, if rather larger in scale, to that of running a successful business in China.

Taking on that challenge will be a task for the future. The question of whether China's entrepreneurs will tackle it is addressed in Chapter 5, as I explore how the endless incremental improvements discussed in this chapter will lead to a transformation of everyday life in China. Before we get there, however, we first need to consider how the innovations that China's entrepreneurs use to survive in their home business environment also prepare them to take on the rest of the world.

4

OUTBOUND

ENTREPRENEURS TO THE WORLD

Over the past decade, people have become used to seeing Chinese companies venture out around the world. However, with a handful of exceptions, these endeavors have been dominated by large state-owned enterprises. They often seem designed to meet government priorities—specifically, to gain access to the resources China needs to keep its economy expanding. Between the early 2000s and 2012, for example, Chinese state-owned companies made energy- and natural resource–related purchases in both developing and developed economies. China's share of global energy and mining acquisitions rose from less than 3 percent to 15 percent per year. One notable deal was the 2008 purchase of a 9 percent stake in Anglo-Australian miner Rio Tinto by Chinalco, the state-owned giant Aluminum Corporation of China. Another was the $15.1 billion purchase of Canada's Nexen in

2013 by China National Offshore Oil Corporation, another state-owned firm—the largest overseas investment by any Chinese company at the time of writing this book.

Just in the last few years, however, the nature of Chinese overseas investment has begun to change—and in a radical way. In 2010, total outbound investment by private Chinese companies was $10 billion, just 15 percent of all China's outbound investment. By 2014, private companies' share of all outbound investment had jumped to 40 percent and its value nearly quadrupled to $49 billion. That change is even more significant than it seems. The money spent by state-owned businesses tends to be spent by relatively few companies in large amounts, whereas the private sector investment comes from many businesses spending, on average, far less on each deal. So the trend is clear: private Chinese companies are starting to move into the world at large en masse, seeking both markets and business acquisitions.

Some of these individual deals are noteworthy as well. In 2014, not only did Henan Province–based pork producer WH Group acquire Smithfield Foods for $7.1 billion, but Dalian Wanda, China's biggest property company, bought the United States's AMC Entertainment for $2.6 billion, overnight making itself the owner of more cinemas worldwide than any other firm.

This move of Chinese entrepreneurship out into other economies is unprecedented in the country's history. Chinese institutions, while dominant within its borders, have not moved far beyond them in the past. Over the next few years, however, a great wave of entrepreneurial companies will pour out of China. They will be looking for new markets, acquisition targets, technology and expertise, and sources of capital.

Much of the money being invested by Chinese companies will go to developed markets, especially the United States. Since the global financial crisis, Chinese investment in the United States has surged, from around $1 billion a year in 2008 and 2009 to more than $14 billion in 2013. Indeed, since 2010, Chinese investment in the United States has well exceeded that of the United States in China.

R&D spending by Chinese-owned firms in the United States has also grown fast, from almost nothing in 2007 to more than $350 million in 2011, and probably approaching half a billion dollars annually by 2014. That is still far from the sums spent by Japanese and German companies, but has already overtaken the amount spent by South Korea and Taiwan.

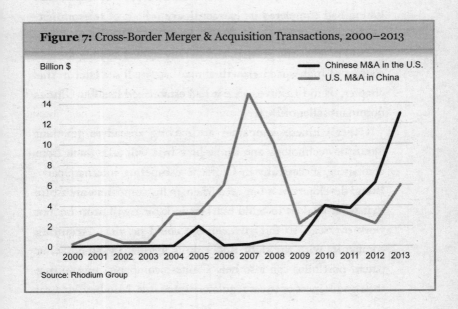

Figure 7: Cross-Border Merger & Acquisition Transactions, 2000–2013

Billion $

— Chinese M&A in the U.S.
— U.S. M&A in China

Source: Rhodium Group

A COMING OF AGE

If there is a single factor underlying this surge in investment by Chinese private companies, it is quite simply a coming of age. Since China joined the World Trade Organization in 2001 and foreign companies flooded into the country, Chinese private enterprises have scrambled to acquire the skills and capabilities necessary to take on multinationals and out-compete their domestic rivals. The principal goal for most of them was to master China's domestic markets and the ever-expanding range of opportunities they offered.

Those lessons have been learned, and companies are looking for new ways of maintaining their momentum. For some, especially those who have built a dominant position at home, finding new markets is a key factor. Huawei and ZTE, for example, once China had completed its extraordinary rollout of telecom networks in the 1990s and 2000s, both struggled to find new sources of domestic growth, and so they started looking for new sources of high-speed growth abroad. As we'll see later in this chapter, so did Lenovo, once it had established itself as China's dominant seller of PCs.

Other Chinese companies are moving abroad to get their hands on technology and know-how that will take them from competing successfully in China to competing internationally. Brand development is one area where many companies are aware that what worked to build markets in China will probably not work overseas, so foreign expertise could be vital. Acquiring companies with the right R&D skills, regulatory expertise, or patent portfolios can also help Chinese companies ensure that their goods meet overseas regulatory standards. Mindray Medical

International, for example, China's largest medical-equipment manufacturer, began its international expansion in 2008 by purchasing the patient monitoring division of New Jersey–based Datascope Corporation for $209 million. That opened the gate for the company to build a portfolio of products approved by the U.S. Food and Drug Administration and other Western regulatory bodies, which in turn have allowed Mindray to expand its operations to some 140 countries.

In addition, in almost all these cases, pride plays a role. The acquirers and investors want to show the world that Chinese companies, or at least *their* company, can be as good as those from any other country.

As outward investment flows continue to grow, China's engagement with the rest of the world is changing. One turning point was the 2008 global financial crisis and subsequent recession, when, with many Western companies struggling to survive, Chinese businesses found themselves able to buy businesses at a fraction of the price they would have had to pay a few years earlier. In 2010, automaker Geely bought Volvo from Ford for $1.5 billion, just 11 years after the American carmaker had acquired the Swedish firm for $6.5 billion. Also in the United States, photovoltaic-cell manufacturer Hanergy has acquired a string of distressed solar-power technology firms, among them Miasolé, Alta Devices, and Global Solar Energy, while in Europe, Shanghai-based conglomerate Fosun spent just over €1 billion (about $1.25 billion) buying Portugal's largest insurance group, Caixa Seguros.

Increasingly, instead of bargain hunting among ailing companies, Chinese buyers are looking for high-end technologies and successful businesses that will help international growth. A few years ago, companies went overseas in search of ways of enhancing their operations in China; secondhand technology, especially bought cheaply, was a good way of doing this. Now they know they need more sophisticated goods and services if they want to enter developed markets, and so they are willing to step up investment in companies that are creating or working with the newest technologies.

Many competitors have been caught by surprise when Chinese entrepreneurs show up in their industry; but as they have entered new markets, those entrepreneurs have often been surprised themselves. Many are discovering that they are better equipped to compete than they expected to be. Their home market-developed strengths can help them both grow and absorb foreign acquisitions. Their ability to react quickly allows them to advance through trial and error, capitalizing where they find a source of advantage while absorbing the cost of their mistakes.

Private companies are also increasingly confident that they can avoid the mistakes made by their predecessors, in particular state-owned Chinese companies, who failed to do their homework and tripped up when moving to compete abroad. They want to avoid calamities such as Citic Pacific and Metallurgical Corporation of China's Sino Iron mine in Western Australia, which as of mid 2014 was four years behind schedule and $6 billion over budget.

LENOVO'S EXPERIENCE

Many of the different motivations driving the global ambitions of Chinese entrepreneurs are brought together at China's most internationally oriented company: Lenovo. A decade ago, at the start of 2005, Lenovo sold one product—personal computers—in one market—China. It was all but unknown outside the country. Today, it is a global power. Not only is it the world's largest PC seller, a title it claimed in 2013 when it displaced Hewlett-Packard, but it is also the world's third-largest seller of smartphones and one of the world's leading sellers of network servers. From its dual headquarters in Beijing and North Carolina, it runs manufacturing and R&D operations in 60 countries, and sells its products in 160.

Lenovo did not make itself the world's biggest personal-computer maker by copying American competitors. Instead, it applied beyond China's borders the practices it developed for China, while, at the same time, consciously redesigning itself to be an international business.

The most important breakthrough for Lenovo came in 2005, with a deal brokered by its CEO, Yang Yuanqing, to buy IBM's money-losing PC division for $1.75 billion. Yang, who had joined Lenovo after graduating from Beijing's University of Science and Technology in 1989 at age 25, had risen fast through the company, becoming the head of its personal-computer arm in 1993. Through the 1990s and early 2000s, he built Lenovo into China's PC market leader, with a 30 percent market share and $3 billion in revenues—enough to ensure that he was appointed CEO when the company's founder, Liu Chuanzhi, stepped down in 2001. By then, with further domestic growth hampered by fierce competition with other Chinese PC makers, Yang set a new goal: making Lenovo an international force.

IBM's decision to sell its PC division gave him that chance. Overnight, the deal quadrupled Lenovo's revenue to $12 billion and made it a global player. The company took ownership of IBM's "Think" family, including its ThinkPad notebook brand, and bought out IBM's interest in its joint venture with domestic rival Great Wall Technology, then China's second-largest PC maker. Lenovo also acquired 10,000 IBM employees, some 2,300 in the United States, mostly product designers, marketers, and sales specialists, and most of the rest in China.

Many observers wondered whether Yang had the expertise to digest his purchase. Initially, their skepticism seemed justified. Yang stepped down as CEO, taking up the chairman position instead. His replacement, American Stephen Ward, a former IBM executive, lasted just several months before the reins were given to William Amelio, who had been president of Dell's operations in Asia Pacific and Japan. Despite talk of growing the company at twice the industry rate, profits failed to materialize as revenue growth remained sluggish, rising a total of just 25 percent over the next four years. Lenovo fell from being the world's third-biggest PC maker to being a distant fourth.

The recession that followed the global financial crisis made things worse. It hit corporate sales badly, while efforts to move into other areas of business all flopped, most notably an effort to launch a mobile phone arm, which Lenovo sold for $100 million to the private-equity arm of its parent, Legend Holdings.

Inside the company, however, Yang was driving a series of major changes. Step-by-step he set about transforming Lenovo from a Chinese company into a global one. He established joint headquarters in Beijing and North Carolina, moving his own primary residence to the United States, and began a concerted drive to close the gap between the company's two different national cultures.

At the same time, he made sure to retain the key strengths of its China operations. As PCs became commodities, Lenovo took full advantage of China's ever-increasing manufacturing strengths, trimming production costs and expanding economies of scale.

In 2009, William Amelio left, and, explicitly promising to shake things up, Yang reinstalled himself as CEO. Adopting the slogan "Protect and attack," he gave Lenovo two priorities. First was protecting sales in China so as to ensure its primary revenue stream remained intact. Second was attacking internationally by finding new sources of high-speed growth in overseas markets around the world.

Yang bought back the mobile-devices business for $200 million, and started pushing the company into tablets and consumer PCs. Up and down the company's supply chain, he forced managers simultaneously to trim costs and upgrade component quality. And he started iterating products in a continuous cycle. By 2013, Lenovo was launching 180 different products annually, from smartphones to its Yoga IdeaPad, a cross between a tablet and a PC.

The strategy paid off. Total revenues more than doubled from $16.6 billion in 2010 to $38.7 billion in 2014. By the end of that period, although revenues were barely rising in Lenovo's home market, they were expanding at nearly 50 percent across Europe, the Middle East, and Africa, and at 20 percent in the Americas.

Now, with the world's PC market in decline—sales have dropped every year since 2011—Lenovo needs to find further new ways of adding both scale and growth. One indicator of its strategy came in early 2014, when, in the space of a week, the company announced it was buying IBM's low-end server business for $2.3 billion and Motorola Mobility from Google for $2.9 billion.

Between them, the two acquisitions should push Lenovo's annual revenues past $50 billion and will also send the company back into the red. (IBM's server business had lost money for seven successive quarters, and Motorola Mobility cost Google more than $1 billion in 2013.)

Yang says he will apply the same cost-cutting techniques Lenovo used to trim expenses at IBM's PC operation. He also says further aggressive acquisitions will be made as part of the company's search for sources of growth beyond its PC business.

Will Lenovo succeed? Certainly Yang will be tested. His company's entry into the smartphone and tablet markets was a major departure from its PC business, bringing a very different set of challenges. The smartphone market in particular is difficult: the market leaders, Apple and Samsung, are both hugely savvy marketers, who between them took all the world's smartphone profits in 2013. Lenovo will also find itself slugging it out with Chinese companies, including Huawei and Xiaomi and a host of other brands, looking to claim a share at the lower end of the smartphone market.

Even before buying Motorola Mobility and IBM's low-end server arm, Lenovo's margins were thin, averaging 1 to 2 percent for the last five years. Now, set to operate in the red while it digests those two purchases, it has little spare money for research into new products and technologies. Moreover, although its products are found in nearly every country around the world, China remains by far its principal market—responsible for nearly 40 percent of its revenues. In the United States, for example, despite its ownership of the ThinkPad brand, its share of the PC market is only 10 percent; HP and Dell both have around 25 percent. There is no guarantee that Lenovo will be able to repeat its successful integration of IBM's personal-computer arm with its purchases of Motorola Mobility or IBM's server business.

Still, Lenovo's progress has been rather like China's—subject at each point along its trajectory to much questioning and skepticism from impatient observers, and yet quite extraordinary in retrospect. It is a far more sophisticated company than it was a decade ago. Its marketing has improved enormously, not just for its smartphones but also for its tablets and high-end PCs. One of its smartest moves was signing up Hollywood star Ashton Kutcher as a "product engineer" to help promote new products. Kutcher, who played Steve Jobs in the *Jobs* movie, also has a strong record as an investor in tech start-ups, among them Skype, Foursquare, and Airbnb.

Even if its purchases of Motorola Mobility and IBM's low-end servers both fail, that wouldn't bring down the company. If they succeed, however, they have the potential to transform Lenovo from a $50 billion company into a $100 billion one.

THE TACTICS OF EXPANSION

Which Chinese companies will be most successful at internationalizing themselves? Experience to date suggests that the global winners will be those that, like Lenovo, combine scale in China, an ability to absorb international practices and management, and access to the funds needed to undertake major international acquisitions.

Some companies will move overseas incrementally, developing their capabilities gradually but in an across-the-board manner.

As with Lenovo, among their goals will be finding new ways of augmenting their current activities rather than pursuing a specific strategic vision. While on the surface this might make them look unfocused, it will help these companies find and develop new ways to add value to existing products and increase sales, particularly in accessible markets, before going worldwide. Many companies will test products in emerging economies first, with the goal of gaining enough experience to move into middle-income countries and eventually into rich ones.

Other companies are going straight to developed markets, typically through mergers and acquisitions. So far, many of the acquisitions by Chinese companies overseas have been in areas where they want to build expertise but which attract little media attention, such as manufacturing and equipment. For example, Sany made itself the world's leading producer of high-technology concrete pumps when it bought Germany's Putzmeister, a family-owned engineering company, in 2012 for €360 million. Another business-to-business international expander is Wanxiang Group, China's biggest auto-components maker, with global revenues of more than $13 billion and a worldwide workforce of more than 45,000 people, including some 3,000 employees in the United States. A private company that can trace its origins back to the late 1960s, when its founder, Lu Guanqiu, started a business making tractor parts, it now runs 26 auto-parts operations in the United States. Its purchases include bankrupt American electric carmaker Fisker Automotive for $149 million in 2013 and an investment of $450 million to keep A123 Systems, a bankrupt maker of electric-car batteries, in operation. Already, one in three cars made in the United States uses auto parts made at a Wanxiang America–owned plant.

GEELY BUYS A BRAND

At the start of 2010, Geely Auto was a minor player in China's auto industry—a mid-sized, privately owned carmaker based in east China's Zhejiang Province. The company was profitable, but with sales of just 400,000 vehicles a year. In March of that year, however, it transformed its scope and reputation overnight with the announcement that it was buying Swedish carmaker Volvo from Ford Motor Company for $1.5 billion.

Five years on, the prospects for Geely's global aspirations remain as uncertain as the day the company struck that audacious deal. And if its gamble does pay off, it could well find itself as China's first global automaker.

The purchase was anything but an obvious prospect for success. Although it more than quadrupled the Chinese carmaker's revenues, and nearly doubled its annual sales volume, it also landed Geely with a company that had been losing money for years. Despite its best efforts, Ford had failed to revive the brand since acquiring it in 1999. Turning it around would require $11 billion, Geely estimated—quite a stretch for a company with an annual turnover of just $3 billion before the Volvo purchase. Geely's founder and owner, Li Shufu, however, was confident he had a solution that would allow him to succeed where Ford had failed, by selling Volvo cars in volume in China.

Li, born in 1963 into a farming family in Zhejiang Province, had been running his own businesses since his teenage years, starting with a photo studio with equipment he made himself. Noticing that photographic by-products included valuable elements such as silver, he started a second business trying to recover valuable metals from discarded equipment. That enterprise went nowhere, so after studying engineering, in the late 1980s, he started a refrigerator components company, which he then upgraded to making whole refrigerators. A change in regulations forced him to hand that business over to the local government. After a second spell at university at age 30, he launched China's first privately owned motorcycle factory in 1993.

His timing was perfect. As Deng Xiaoping's relaunch of economic reforms took hold, people across China abandoned their bicycles for motorbikes, and by the mid 1990s Li was running one of China's biggest private companies. Fifteen years later, it was an automaker with giant aspirations.

During the first few years after the Volvo acquisition, things didn't work out as Li had planned. He had expected that his company, already China's biggest non-state-owned carmaker, would parlay its new access to a globally recognized brand name and advanced automotive technology into a major position in the country's burgeoning motor-vehicle market. But Chinese government officials, who had long wanted to see the country's state-owned auto firms emerge as national leaders, were clearly uncomfortable with the deal. They ruled that, despite Geely's 100 percent ownership of Volvo, the government would continue to treat Volvo as a foreign company. If Geely wanted to make and sell Volvo cars in China, it would have to form a joint venture with its own subsidiary.

Though sales of Geely cars rose steadily to 700,000 by 2013, its Volvo arm continued to struggle. Although production rose enough for it to finally hit its break-even target in 2013, plans for annual sales of 200,000 of its cars in China by 2015 were clearly far too ambitious. Despite China's total car sales rising more than 5 million units from 2010 to 2015, sales of Volvos were just 81,000 in 2014.

None of this fazed Li. He acquired more troubled foreign auto companies, buying Manganese Bronze, the money-losing UK-based maker of London's black taxis, and Australia-based Drivetrain Systems International, a bankrupt maker of automatic transmissions. And he started spending heavily on electric vehicles. He put Geely and Volvo together to work on developing a plug-in hybrid car; established a $160 million electric car joint venture with Kandi Technologies Group, another private Chinese company based in Zhejiang; signed a partnership agreement with Michigan-based Detroit Electric to produce electric cars for sale in China; and bought the UK electric car start-up Emerald Automotive with a promise to invest $200 million over five years.

Whether Li has laid the foundations for a sustainable, long-term business is hard to gauge, but certainly all of the opportunities and challenges faced by Chinese companies attempting to go global are evident, in particular whether they can assemble operations in a way that can create a larger whole.

His total exports, now running at around 150,000 cars a year, barely register on the global scale. None of those sales are in developed countries, nor are they likely to be for at least several years. And being China's best-selling private carmaker doesn't even get it into the list of the country's top 10 auto sellers by market share. (In 2013, those were Volkswagen, General Motors, Hyundai, Renault/Nissan, Chang'an, Toyota, Ford, BAIC, Dongfeng, and Honda; the three Chinese companies on the list are all state-owned enterprises.) Yet Li's achievements with Geely are as striking as those of any entrepreneur profiled in this book. With little official support, he has assembled a set of global auto assets, along the way acquiring enough electric vehicle expertise to give him the option of moving in that direction if demand warrants it. Though Volvo continues to be a troubled brand in Europe and America, Li could still continue moving Geely up the value chain away from the low-cost entry-level vehicles that every other private Chinese carmaker has made their staple product.

The odds, of course, remain stacked against him, both in China, the world's most bitterly contested car market, and internationally, especially as he has yet to answer the question of how Geely can find the billions of dollars even Li forecasts are needed to revive Volvo. Still, it is no longer a wildly alien notion that a Chinese company could establish itself as a world leader in any major industry. Wanxiang is doing it with the components that go into cars.

If Geely fails, then perhaps BYD may take its place. The Shenzhen-based carmaker already has a plant in California making electric buses and has well-developed plans to have four cars available in 2015. And Chery, the country's other leading private carmaker, is running nine plants of its own around the world. Chery is also in a joint venture with Israel's Israel Corporation as a first step toward entering the European market.

A BREEDING GROUND FOR INTERNATIONAL FIRMS

The final stage in China's evolution to an exporter of companies will occur when its businesses are no longer primarily Chinese. You'll know the transition is complete when these companies, like many American ones today, have substantial facilities around the world, and when they are principally responsive to the demands of the various markets in which they operate rather than always looking to channel back funding and personnel to assist their China business.

Chinese Internet companies are leading the way in this stage with a host of recent purchases in Silicon Valley. Tencent has spent more than $2 billion on overseas acquisitions since 2011, with purchases including American video-game publishers Riot Games for $231 million, and a 48 percent stake in Epic Games for $330 million. It has invested in messaging company Snapchat, giving itself an entrance into the U.S. smartphone communications market as it looks to extend the reach of WeChat around the world. And it has also invested in several venture capital funds so as to have access to news about fast-growing start-ups that it might be able to introduce to China.

Alibaba's interest in American companies has also grown rapidly. Even before its New York listing, its U.S. investment team had spent more than $500 million buying minority stakes in shipping service Shoprunner, mobile messaging application Tango, luxury e-commerce business 1stDibs, and travel-sharing business Lyft.

As they internationalize, Chinese companies will hire an ever greater number and range of foreign executives and other staff who can bring expertise unavailable in China. These people will bring knowledge of how to structure and run global operations, how to develop capabilities where Chinese business are currently weak such as marketing, and how best to enter markets such as the United States that are very different from China's. In return, these people will get to work with some of the world's fastest-growing and most dynamic businesses.

Again, China's Internet companies are leading the way on this front. In Chapter 1, I noted how Joe Tsai was one of Jack Ma's first key hires at Alibaba. Tencent has also brought in executives with experience abroad, including company president Martin Lau, who worked at McKinsey before moving to Goldman Sachs to run its Asia telecom, media, and technology group; chief strategy officer James Mitchell, who also worked at Goldman Sachs, heading up its global Internet coverage in New York before joining Tencent in 2011; and David Wallerstein, an American who joined the organization in 2001 and now oversees its international business initiatives. Other types of businesses are following this lead. Huawei's Shenzhen-based rival, ZTE, another company looking to expand by establishing itself as a smartphone maker, has hired staff from troubled Western telecom firms such as Canada's BlackBerry and Motorola Mobility.

THE POWER OF PRIVATE COMPANIES

Looking into the future, although state-owned companies will continue to venture overseas, their share of Chinese global investment will decline. One reason for this is simply poor performance: due to a combination of inexperience and a lack of accountability, many state-owned companies heavily overpaid for their purchases and then had trouble digesting them. In 2005, for example, Nanjing Auto bought the UK's MG Rover for an undisclosed sum. Two years later, with Nanjing Auto selling less than 80,000 cars annually, it off-loaded its purchase to Shanghai-based SAIC Motor Corp, another state-owned company and a partner of both GM and Volkswagen in their China joint ventures. Sales of MG cars in the UK were negligible over the next several years—in 2012, totaling just 782, despite SAIC having invested more than $500 million. In China it has fared a little better, though sales in 2013 were only 75,000 for its MG marque and 155,000 for its Roewe brand, established to sell cars based on the Rover platform acquired as part of the MG deal.

State-owned companies are also reluctant to bring in executives from outside, and have often proved insensitive in their dealings with local populations, causing major reputational damage to both themselves and China. In Africa, a big rise in Chinese trade and investment has had a mixed reception. Governments across the continent have been pleased at China's willingness to fund infrastructure projects, but resentment has also arisen at the many workers brought in from China to help build them, leading to protests and riots in Zambia, Angola, and Congo.

Moreover, China's economy is moving away from an investment-driven, energy-intensive model to one that emphasizes increasing productivity. While the government wants state-owned companies to become more efficient, incentivizing them to change is difficult: organizations such as China's big energy and resource companies thrive on scale and their ability to control resources.

Finally, because of their split loyalties, it is unlikely that more than a handful of China's state-owned companies will ever develop a truly global identity. As arms of the state, they are charged by definition with advancing Chinese national interests.

The government seems to be recognizing this. Through 2012 and 2013, it quietly increased the level of official support offered to private companies going abroad. Previously, only a few privileged such firms—mostly infrastructure-related ones such as Huawei and ZTE, or ones with particularly close official ties, such as carmaker Chery—had received help with export finance or loans to build overseas factories.

Now, however, ever more private companies are finding that they too can receive help when they need it. In 2012, China Development Bank signed an agreement with Fosun to provide the Shanghai-based conglomerate with $3.85 billion in development finance, much of it earmarked to buy struggling businesses in developed countries.

Even Geely, long spurned by the central government, has begun to receive official support. In 2013, China Development Bank promised Li Shufu support to help Volvo open its second and third factories in China. And in early 2014, Export-Import Bank of China granted Geely a $3.2 billion credit line to help fund its overseas expansion. "As a state financial institution, China ExIm Bank sees it as our responsibility to help Chinese companies expand overseas," the bank noted, according to Britain's *Financial Times*.

UP THE LEARNING CURVE

When it comes to international presence, China still has some catching up to do. Today, its annual outward investment is still smaller than Japan's and less than one-third of America's, while its total overseas stock is less than one-tenth of the United States's or Europe's. But the same spirit and ambition that has driven Chinese entrepreneurs on at home is starting to send them overseas, into new markets and new industries, and at an accelerating rate.

Entrepreneurs heading overseas face a steep learning curve. But as China has opened up and the barriers to international business have fallen, they and their companies have been exposed to global business practices. Though they may still be novices when it comes to running operations across several countries, their ability to search for and adopt new practices continually, combined with a high tolerance for risk, will result in their global presence growing much faster than most people anticipate.

As more private companies head overseas, the visibility of Chinese products and services will grow. We can guess which sectors are most likely to lead. Smartphones by Xiaomi, Lenovo, or Huawei could be first, followed by cars. China's leading Internet companies could expand aggressively. Alibaba, helped by its spectacularly successful initial public offering in September 2014, has the firepower to be an international force, especially if it continues with the acquisition spree it conducted ahead of its flotation. Tencent already has a significant presence in the United States thanks to its investments in other companies and in WeChat has the potential to become a global powerhouse. Tencent spent $200 million promoting WeChat overseas in both 2013 and 2014. Likewise, Robin Li's Baidu is making a concerted push into new markets, launching a Portuguese-language version of its search service in Brazil in mid 2014 that is aimed at attracting new users in a country where Internet penetration is still low rather than persuading existing ones to abandon Google.

As Chinese companies go overseas, they will take their

China-developed capabilities with them. Around the world, businesses will find themselves facing Chinese companies using their domestic-market strengths as a springboard to enter foreign markets. The Chinese will be bolstered by their unrivaled economies of scale, as well as the flexibility and resourcefulness forced on them by an environment demanding constant iteration and change. They will be tough competitors in any market. Huawei has demonstrated this with its telecom-network equipment; Lenovo, in a different way, with its PC-centered model.

The global growth of China's entrepreneurs represents the next stage in China's transition to being a global economic superpower. As private companies look certain to continue increasing both their share of China's outbound investment and, more significantly, their total spending, China will become a net global investor, possibly as soon as 2017, according to a study by the UK's Economist Intelligence Unit. By then, its total yearly outbound investment figure will be more than $170 billion, second only in volume to the United States.

This achievement will mark a significant turning point in China's economic trajectory. For most of the more than three decades since Deng Xiaoping opened the Chinese economy to the world, inbound foreign direct investment was the key driver of growth—funding the building of China's export economy and supplying much of the technology now used to power the economy. At this juncture it will be Chinese companies heading overseas that will create growth opportunities in other countries—building factories, creating jobs, and boosting output.

In a world in which China is the second-biggest—and soon to be the biggest—economy, this expansion of global reach of its companies should in theory be regarded as a natural next step.

While they pose a threat, if China's leading entrepreneurial companies can make themselves into international companies, then the benefits could also be enormous—not just for China, but around the world. China will become a global innovation engine, one of several in the world. Just as Japanese entrepreneurs benefited the world when they went overseas, and Koreans did after them, the Chinese company diaspora will become a major force for innovation and economic revitalization.

In the long term, the emergence of a world where investment between China and the rest of the world is genuinely a two-way process will benefit everyone. A richer Chinese market will offer companies from other countries opportunities too—directly or via the opportunity to invest in Chinese companies—while consumers around the world will benefit from the innovations and goods made by Chinese companies.

5

CHANGING CHINA

In February 2013, Victor Wang, the chairman of Mtone Wireless, one of the first companies to launch mobile Internet services in China, stood up to give a talk to a group of several hundred of his peers. The setting was a four-day meeting of the China Entrepreneurs Forum (CEF), the country's most powerful private business organization, hosted every winter at Yabuli, a ski resort in northeast China. Wang opened by summarizing China's changes during the previous three decades. Everyone knew that China had urbanized, become a part of the global economy, and moved online. But did they know that its entrepreneurs and their businesses had increased their share of economic output from nothing to two-thirds of GDP and now accounted for 60 percent of taxes and nearly 9 out of 10 jobs?

For the country's development to continue, Wang went on, a transformation in governance was necessary. Over the next 30 years, China would need to make a clear transition toward the rule of law and the development of a civil society with multiple voices and points of view. In this scenario, the government would no longer be the sole authority determining how China was run, but would be guided by social entrepreneurs, think tanks, and mature nongovernment organizations (NGOs), both from China and overseas. And if these changes weren't made? The cost of sticking with its current ways was unsustainable, Wang said, putting up a slide with an image of an old-fashioned bomb.

To people observing China from a distance, this might have seemed like an inflammatory statement—or a naïve one. Certainly it seems like advocacy for political change of the sort that the Chinese government condemns. But his comments and the enthusiastic way in which they were received by his fellow entrepreneurs represent a new reality in China, which few outsiders have noticed or understand.

Wang is like many Chinese entrepreneurs today; his views on China's future direction are subtle and multifaceted. He has a genuine love of his country and a respect for his country's government. Yet he is absolutely sincere about the reforms he seeks, and he feels he has the right to influence the state—in fact, that he and his peers have a duty to combine the wealth and influence they have acquired with a sense of responsibility for the well-being of society. Speaking on a separate occasion, he noted that ensuring China's peaceful transition to a modern nation with the rule of law and individual autonomy, avoiding turmoil and minimizing chaos along the way, was an "inescapable historical responsibility."

Wang's view is noteworthy for the way in which he expresses it. He doesn't advocate change in China's political system, but rather that the needs of its entrepreneurs and others should be accommodated within the current system. Of course, doing so would over time change the balance of power within that system. But phrased this way, it's a more subtle way of sending a message: not that China needs to see the emergence of a rounded civil society and well-developed legal system in order to advance, but rather that private companies are already driving changes that could only be reversed at the cost of endangering the very developmental goals the government wants to pursue. In other words, for China to prosper, its entrepreneurs must prosper too. For this to happen, officials must switch from tacitly accepting them, as was largely the case from 2002 to 2012, when China was run by Hu Jintao and Wen Jiabao, to actively supporting entrepreneurialism.

The gatherings of the CEF, especially its winter meeting at Yabuli, but also its summer gatherings held at different locations, are one leading venue for this type of discussion in China. These meetings bring together many of China's richest and most influential private business owners gather for a program that mixes skiing, talks on business and economic topics, dinners, and informal discussions. Other economic meetings in China may be better known; for example, the Boao forum where leaders from Asian governments convene, or the World Economic Forum's China meetings held in Dalian and Tianjin. But the Yabuli forum might be the most important event of its kind in Asia, because it is a forum for entrepreneurs to discuss their larger influence on the country's systems.

The forum was informally launched in 2000 when Wang Wei, the founder of China's first mergers and acquisitions firm, China M&A Group, and economist Lawrence Tian, the founder of China's first futures company, China International Futures Corporation, brought together a group of friends and officials for a short conference. Its key driving force since the founding has been Chen Dongsheng, who, as we saw in Chapter 1, is the founder of China's largest privately owned insurance company, Taikang Life Insurance. After becoming the CEF's chairman in 2002, he transformed the forum from a private, social gathering to a publicly engaged body with an agenda, reorganizing its finances and memberships, and encouraging attendance by requiring all members who miss meetings for a year to pay a fine of 100,000 yuan (roughly $15,000). He also launched a research foundation, funded at first by an auction of wine donated by members, and made promoting a better business environment for private companies the federation's explicit goal.

For the first several years, membership was strictly restricted. Many members came from the Gang of '92, the group of entrepreneurs who left jobs in government and academia after Deng Xiaoping launched China's second wave of economic reforms in 1992. Indeed, even by 2010, the CEF only had 50 members, though they included many of the figures behind China's most powerful companies, including Alibaba's Jack Ma; Lenovo's Yang Yuanqing; Guo Wei of Digital China, one of China's leading IT companies; Li Dongsheng of TCL, one of China's biggest electronics firms; Guo Guangchang, chairman of China's biggest privately owned conglomerate, Shanghai Fosun Group; Feng Lun of Vantone; Wang Shi from property developer Vanke; and Zhang Yue, whose Broad Group, an air-conditioning and construction company, is profiled in this book's final chapter.

The organization has grown in the last few years, though even today its membership remains at just a few hundred. The vast majority of those who attend are practicing entrepreneurs who know each other well, and their discussions remain focused on what can be done to protect and advance the interests of private business. Significantly, each meeting is also attended by senior central and provincial government officials, figures such as Jiang Jianqing, the chairman of ICBC, China's largest state-owned bank; Liu Mingkang, the former chairman of the China Banking Regulatory Commission; and Ding Xuedong, the head of China Investment Corporation, the country's sovereign wealth fund.

Most discussions at Yabuli center on business and economic issues. But since the start, broader themes have also consistently been broached: the damage China's development has done to its natural environment, the broader responsibilities entrepreneurs have toward society, or, as in Wang's case, the nature of the changes China is undergoing and where they might lead.

Buttressing Wang's argument are the changes private companies are forcing in the economy—not just in establishing successful businesses, but in recasting the ways in which key industries operate. Take finance, health care, and the media. All three sectors have traditionally been state-run, and the government continues to regard each as a strategic area that it is responsible for and wants to control. Yet in each of these industries, despite continuing restrictions, entrepreneurs are finding opportunities and reworking regulatory boundaries in ways that advance the government's broader goals for developing China.

REACHING CHINA'S NEW RICH

In finance, we have already seen how Alibaba is transforming saving and widening the lending opportunities available to small and medium-sized businesses. Another company changing this sector is Noah Wealth Management, a Shanghai-based money-management firm serving China's fast-growing high-net-worth population.

Noah's founder, Wang Jingbo, was born in 1972 in Sichuan. After completing a bachelor's degree in economics and a master's degree in management at Chengdu's Sichuan University, she moved to Shanghai in 1992 to work in the city's financial industry, which had recently opened its first post-Mao stock market. In 2000, she joined Xiangcai Securities, one of China's leading securities firms, first to head up its asset management department, then as deputy head of its joint-venture fund management business, formed with Holland's ABN AMRO. From 2003 to 2005, she ran its private banking arm.

At that time, China's wealth management business had lost its way. Despite the economy steaming ahead, the country's stock markets were going through an extended bad patch that had led to all initial public offerings being suspended for two years. Xiangcai decided to exit private banking. Rather than see the business shut down, Wang took over the business, launching it as Noah in 2005.

A pair of angel investors helped Noah through its first months, allowing Wang to establish enough of a foothold to persuade American venture capital firm Sequoia Capital to invest $4.5 million in 2007. Using this money, she expanded the company's network by more than 60 branches over the next six years, which in turn enabled Noah to sign up more than 50,000 of China's rich, who have invested 113 billion yuan (about $18 billion) through her company, almost all in China.

To protect itself from the possibility of handling money

acquired from graft, Noah does no business with officials. Instead, it focuses on the fast-growing segment of self-made business-people and traders, mostly in their 40s, 50s, or 60s. Current estimates of high-net-worth individuals (HNWIs) in China put the total at between 700,000 and 1.4 million people, with estimates of their total wealth ranging from $3.5 trillion to $5 trillion. The number of HNWIs has doubled since 2008, and is now increasing by around 20 percent a year, while their wealth is growing even faster. They can be found across China (some 20 provinces have more than 10,000, according to Bain & Co.), but Shanghai is home to their biggest concentration, with about 30 percent of the national total.

Noah's success is just the tip of an iceberg. At the start of 2014, total assets managed by China's wealth management industry were worth 11 trillion yuan (about $1.8 trillion) and growing at 65 percent a year, according to Standard Chartered, a British bank headquartered in Hong Kong.

The reason for this astonishing growth rate is not only the proliferation of high-net-worth individuals, but the emergence of the consuming classes discussed in Chapter 1. The products pioneered by Noah and other financial services companies may have originally been aimed at China's richest individuals, but they are now being adapted to meet the broader needs of ordinary savers, those that Alibaba and Tencent are targeting with their Internet-based money-market products.

This presents the government with a challenge. Should it clamp down on such products or encourage them? Stronger regulation is undoubtedly necessary as the level of risk involved in investing in these products remains far from clear. Inevitably some of them will be tested, quite possibly leading to one or more of the institutions behind them failing—leading either to investors losing money or, more likely, an officially organized bailout.

But too much interference would also cause problems, penalizing investors who finally have found ways of earning better returns on their savings and discouraging the private consumption that broader policy goals aim to stimulate. The likely response, therefore, is step-by-step liberalization.

Interest-rate liberalization, for example, would encourage banks to price and allocate capital more efficiently and lead to companies, especially state-owned ones, being less wasteful. Credit would flow to previously underserved industries and companies, particularly private ones, and the range of financial products would also expand.

This is the most probable route that Xi Jinping's government will take in the next several years. And as it does, it will create opportunities for more and more entrepreneurs like Wang Jingbo to develop a market segment that was nonexistent just five years ago. But these companies, as well as reacting to the wealth that is being created in China by finding ways of offering services that bring benefits to the country's new rich, are also shaping things.

These start-ups, while gently forcing the government's hand, are almost certain to be allowed to continue. Thanks to its control over China's main macroeconomic levers, the government retains the power to act whenever necessary. It can support exporters by manipulating the value of the yuan; through its capital controls, it can prevent money entering or leaving the country in destabilizing volumes; and, if necessary, it can stimulate short-term growth by making funding freely available through the state-owned banking system. Beyond this, it willingly allows private companies a largely free hand. Doing so promotes goals that the government wants to realize in the long run. By creating new products and services, consumers get both more choice and the opportunity of higher returns. This in turn encourages the increased private consumption that the government hopes can replace state-financed capital investment as the main driver of economic growth. Private companies also increase the pressure on state-owned companies and banks to improve their performance, in turn encouraging a better allocation of resources and so in the long term contributing to higher levels of productivity.

Over the years, new private vehicles for wealth management will inevitably erode the government's control over the financial system, but that is precisely the point. What China needed through the 1990s and 2000s was to be able to direct money into infrastructure and construction. What it needs through the rest of this decade and beyond is investment that raises productivity. Ultimately, commercial financial organizations will be the best judges of where money should be directed. To attract the funds of Noah's investors or of the ordinary savers putting their money into Yu'e Bao, Alibaba's online money-market fund, these companies will have to be better at finding the right investment opportunities. With the rise of private finance businesses, we are seeing the start of this shift.

HELPING HEALTH CARE

A similar process is unfolding in health care. Although China's system will remain very much a publicly run system for the foreseeable future, private companies are extending the quality and range of services.

The next decade will see a radical change as China adopts supply-side liberalization, with many new services coming from private companies in what is likely to be one of China's biggest areas of service sector growth. Opportunities for private sector health-care providers in particular will grow fast, pushed by surging demand from the nation's wealthy for high-end services, and the challenges posed by a rapidly aging population.

Thanks to reforms carried out in the first decade of this century, China now has near-universal health-insurance coverage. Though the level isn't high, especially for rural families, the share of out-of-pocket cash expenditures in total health spending has fallen to around 35 percent from a peak of 60 percent. The government is now focusing on the supply side: training doctors and nurses, lowering drug costs, and raising reimbursement rates. These measures should bring basic treatment within everyone's reach, and in the process encourage people to lower their savings rate and increase their consumption.

As well as increased official spending, the government has also opened health care to both private and foreign investment. As a result, the number of for-profit hospitals has doubled in less than a decade to more than 6,000, with the goal of a 20 percent market share by 2015.

Rising standards of living have raised many Chinese people's expectations of the kind of treatments they have a right to receive. Hospitals are also eager to offer more treatments. But as with health-care systems around the world, costs are spiraling. Further, as China's population ages over the next two decades, both demand and costs will continue to rise relentlessly.

A lot of the changes in efficiency and effectiveness will be governed by health-care officials. Improvements in quality, however, and in particular the introduction of new medical technologies, are creating opportunities for entrepreneurial private companies to raise standards and make money.

How private companies are driving improvements in standards can be seen with the experience of Chen Haibin and his Hangzhou-based company, Dian Diagnostics, which runs a chain of medical laboratories across China with an annual turnover of more than $1 billion.

Chen founded his business in 1996 using imported equipment to offer molecular diagnostic services. Thanks to his experience helping Fosun establish its molecular diagnosis business, sales grew rapidly at Dian Diagnostics during its first two years. "For many people, making the first million is hard," says Chen. "But for me it was quite easy."

In 1998, however, the newly founded State Food and Drug Administration (now known as the China Food and Drug Administration) suspended the use of a wide range of materials pending approval, among them the reagents used by Dian. Overnight, Chen's revenues collapsed.

He cut his staff from 70 people to fewer than 20, then set about reinventing his business as a distributor of diagnostic products made by Roche Diagnostics, an arm of Swiss health-care company Hoffman–La Roche. He vowed never again to allow Dian to be vulnerable to a similar change in policy.

After a tour of hospitals and other health-care operations in Hong Kong and Singapore, he decided to test the market for an independent testing service, spending 5 million yuan (about $600,000 at the time) to set up a trial laboratory. With all medical testing in China conducted by hospitals and clinics in-house, many of his colleagues were skeptical about its prospects. To educate hospitals and clinics about the benefits of independent labs, Chen invited doctors and other medical staff to a forum introducing Dian's services. Assisted by China's National Clinical Laboratory announcing it would be restricting its role to monitoring the quality of laboratories across the country and not doing tests itself, Chen's new business flourished, signing up more than 30 hospitals within days of its launch, and breaking even within a year.

The decision to broaden Dian's business paid off in 2005. That year, in a bid to reduce costs, the government announced it was cutting its reimbursements to hospitals for the drugs they prescribed. Hospitals, in turn, were forced to cut back on drugs, especially costly ones from overseas. This hit Dian's distribution of Roche Diagnostics hard, and a second time, Chen found himself going from running a profitable company to running a money-losing one overnight.

But while the new policy badly damaged Dian's distribution business, it simultaneously boosted demand for its laboratory services, as hospitals, also deprived of income from drug sales, found themselves forced to outsource more tasks, including testing work.

With demand rising sharply, Chen started expanding his network of laboratories. In 2009, needing extra resources to sustain its growth, he sold stakes in Dian to Shanghai-based conglomerate Fosun and Japan's Softbank, and two years later floated the company on the Shenzhen Stock Exchange.

Since then, the constant expansion of Dian's product range has given hospitals access to an ever-greater range of tests developed at no expense or risk to themselves. As of 2014, the company ran a network of 14 labs across China, with plans to add another 16 within the next two years.

Dian is now expanding its research and development facilities with the goal of developing proprietary tests that it can use to supplement those bought in from other companies. It is also looking at ways to extend its scope by adding imaging centers to its range of laboratories, and branching into new areas such as environmental testing.

More recent reforms in Chinese health care have worked in Dian's favor, most notably the 2013 announcement of a switch in policy opening up much of the medical market to investment by private and foreign companies. The old system had stymied growth and encouraged abuse—with officials granting permission on a company-by-company basis, some companies bribed officials to keep competitors off their patch.

China's health-care system will remain predominantly public for the foreseeable future, despite the advances provided by companies such as Dian. But with government policy increasingly encouraging the expansion of private health-care services, as Chen has shown, entrepreneurs will play a key role in transforming China's health-care system, making it more efficient and expanding its scope.

PUSHING AT THE BOUNDARIES OF EXPRESSION

If the changes driven by entrepreneurs in finance and health care are essentially about extending and improving existing systems, those happening in China's media industry look likely to result in a far more radical restructuring.

For decades, because of their influence on public attitudes, China's broadcasting, films, and publishing sectors have been under the tightest controls. China remains a country where state-run broadcasters and publishers dominate the dissemination of news. However, these organizations no longer enjoy the monopoly on information and entertainment they had a decade ago. The government has encouraged a massive growth in entertainment, giving almost everyone something they want to watch, read, or listen to. Sports and soap operas are both popular. Until recently most of this programming was fed to homes via provincially run cable-television networks. But the rise of broadband networks, and especially mobile broadband ones, is leading to a fundamental shift in the way people consume content. One study of Chinese television and online video habits in 2013 found that nearly half of respondents—and an even higher proportion among those under 30—no longer watched television, spending all their viewing time on the Internet.

This online video market is fragmented, with Baidu, Tencent, and the country's biggest portal, Sohu, all having well-established online video arms. But the biggest and most interesting company in this space is Youku Tudou, which takes around 40 percent of the market. Youku Tudou is China's answer to YouTube (which is blocked in the country). Its monthly viewership reached 500 million unique visitors in August 2014, about half YouTube's total, while its revenues—$500 million in 2013—are just one-seventh of YouTube's total income, though with China's online video industry forecast to double in value to 37 billion yuan between 2014 and 2016, that gap will close.

Victor Koo, the founder and CEO of Youku Tudou, was born in Hong Kong to parents from mainland China. Raised speaking

Cantonese, Mandarin, and English, he studied first at boarding school in Australia and then at the University of California–Berkeley in the United States. After working for Bain & Co. for three years, he earned an MBA at Stanford Business School and, in 1994, moved to Beijing to work with venture capital firm Richina Group.

In 1999, with China's Internet barely in existence, he joined Sohu. During his six years at the portal, he guided it to a Nasdaq listing. But like many other entrepreneurial spirits in China, he wanted his own business, and in 2005 he left to set up Youku.

Over the next eight years, the company expanded enough to secure a listing on the New York Stock Exchange in 2010, raising $200 million. The biggest single event of its history to date was a billion-dollar merger in 2012 with rival Tudou.com, then China's second-biggest online video service. The enlarged company has spent heavily, buying rights to popular Chinese television dramas and other professional content.

As with most of China's Internet companies (apart from Tencent), advertising is Youku Tudou's main source of income, accounting for 90 percent of its revenues, though it is trying to increase income from other sources, including selling rights to show its original programming and subscriptions.

Although the merger of Youku and Tudou brought some benefits from greater economies of scale, particularly for equipment costs, increased spending on content acquisition meant that, after briefly breaking even in the last quarter of 2013, Youku resumed its money-losing ways in 2014.

Youku Tudou's future almost certainly lies on the mobile Internet. With daily views rising to 400 million, it is already used more on mobile devices than on computers. By early 2014, consumers were watching around 45 billion minutes a month on the Youku App mobile video application, making it China's third most popular mobile app, after Tencent's WeChat and QQ messaging apps.

Youku spends around 35 to 40 percent of revenues on content, with a growing proportion going to produce in-house content, including a comedy series called *Surprise*, developed using big-data analytic tools that drew 22 million viewers a month. User-generated content on the site has grown steadily, with the highest-earning creators now able to earn at least 80,000 yuan (about $13,000) a month on a regular basis. Explicitly taking a cue from Netflix, the company launched its own movie production company in August 2014 and released 20 new original television series in September. "Our subscriber base," Koo told *Variety*, "is small, but growing in triple digits year by year."

The burgeoning popularity of online entertainment places Youku and its rivals under close government scrutiny. Official media reports have suggested that some 2 million "public opinion analysts," divided between the Communist Party's propaganda department, state-owned news Web sites, and other companies, monitor content and posts to make sure no sensitive material appears, or if it does, that it is taken down as soon as possible.

Every day, the government's propaganda department issues instructions to companies telling them how to handle sensitive topics, for example, by only using reports from government news organs. Under Xi Jinping, the government has tightened its control over Internet discussions, announcing in mid 2013 that anyone who posted defamatory comments viewed by 5,000 other users or reposted more than 500 times could be jailed for up to three years. As part of a government campaign aimed at reining in discussions on China's microblogs, the propaganda department also targeted some of China's most prominent independent bloggers, among them Charles Xue, a venture capitalist with 12 million followers of his Weibo account. Police detained him for eight months, allegedly for soliciting prostitutes, but many people believe that the real reason was the way he and other popular commentators were undermining official power to control public opinion.

Such measures have dampened discussion across the Chinese Internet, though without doing any harm to the business interests of the main Internet companies. However, they are unlikely to stop Internet companies pushing at the boundaries of China's media industry. The government will hit back periodically with restrictions, such as ones announced in September 2014 restricting the amount of foreign-sourced programming shown on online video services to 30 percent of programming. But the variety and volume of entertainment can only increase, pulled by demand as more people acquire smartphones, tablets, and other ways of accessing the Internet.

What are the limits beyond which companies in sensitive industries cannot go in China? The answer depends upon the circumstances, of course. But in most cases, such companies know where the boundaries lie and make sure they remain well within them, largely because they see their interests as broadly aligned with those of the government. "There's no incentive for us to be a force for unrest," says Youku Tudou CEO Koo. As a quid pro quo for commercial freedom, companies such as his, Tencent, Baidu, and others with user-based content routinely acquiesce, hiring staff to monitor their services and remove posts on sensitive subjects as soon as they find it.

Certainly if the government continues its censorship practices, and especially if it becomes more stringent, significant questions will be raised about the long-term prospects of China's Internet companies. Many Western observers say their concerns about monitoring content are a reason for doubt. To them, a company with international ambitions can't afford to be seen as censoring itself or as tracking its people on behalf of a restrictive regime. Within the companies, however, the perspective is rather different. They see themselves participating in a continual process of negotiation that allows them to continue growing their business. There would be no point in jeopardizing services being used by tens or hundreds of millions of people, especially when, over the last three decades, people in China have gained access to an ever-broadening range of information sources.

Moreover, the biggest struggle ahead for Youku Tudou and the rest of China's leading Internet companies will be with each other, not with the government. Youku's dominance, for one, is being threatened by Baidu-backed iQiyi.com and Tencent. To strengthen its position, it took a $1.2 billion investment from Alibaba in April 2014, and seven months later announced that Lei Jun's Xiaomi would be buying a stake in the company as part of his strategy of expanding the Internet video content available to buyers of his smartphones and other devices. The media landscape is evolving too fast for anyone to make plausible forecasts of how it will appear in even five years' time. All that seems certain is that the industry remains in flux, maybe even more so, if only because the mobile Internet is about to become China's biggest entertainment source.

PRESSURING THE STATE

Across the areas explored in this chapter—finance, health care, and the media—private companies will put pressure on both state companies and the government. Banks will have to compete; the health-care system will become more market-oriented, with the needs of users, be they patients or health-care providers, increasingly met by private companies; and private companies will be the primary content deliverers supplying video entertainment to most of the country's population.

While state companies can perform well at such fundamental tasks as building basic infrastructure, they are far weaker when it comes to undertaking the "creative destruction" (as Joseph Schumpeter called it) that an innovative economy requires. This involves the ceaseless testing of new products and processes conducted via a relentless churn of businesses, most of which fail. It also involves the relentless competition for consumer attention, which will inevitably be drawn by those businesses that offer access to information or services that state-owned companies do not provide.

So while the state sector remains powerful and well supported from above, its prospects have started to decline. Its profits as a share of GDP peaked in 2007. Over the next few years, it was artificially supported as the government poured funds into the economy to keep growth going through the global financial crisis. To get the country through a tricky period, that strategy was just right, but now the government has the problem of cleaning things up. Many industries suffer from overcapacity, notably steel, coal mining, aluminum smelting, and cement. Those regions which benefited disproportionately from state largesse from 2008 through 2010 are those which are suffering now.

From now on, state-owned enterprises will find life harder. As well as having less access to cheap finance and other subsidies, the November 2013 plenum also called for 30 percent of all state-owned enterprise profits to be passed on to the government. Pressure from greater market forces will be relentless. Interest-rate deregulation will squeeze banks and their state-owned clients.

The state will be far from absent in all this. It will continue to drive development by investing in infrastructure, education, and research, and direct the giant state-owned enterprises overseeing the economy's most strategic elements. Indeed, I think it is certain that the government will continue to regard itself as the most important force setting the direction of China's development.

But private companies will be responsible for driving things such as improving the standard and variety of services, introducing competition where this can act as an incentive to make operations more efficient, and meeting unserved needs such as those of small- and medium-sized enterprises. And—possibly of even greater significance in the long term—entrepreneurs will also be responsible for introducing a very different way of organizing not just businesses but also everyday life. The rise of the mobile Internet and the impact it is having on all manner of service businesses—from retailing and finance to entertainment, education, and health care—will lead to the spread of an Internet mind-set—an outlook on life based on the principles of transparency and openness. At the enterprise level, this will lead to ever greater decentralization, with business units closest to customers having to take ever greater responsibility for decisions, and acquiring the means to debate and shape them. Whether such practices could ultimately spill over into other areas of life remains very much unknown, but there is clearly a degree of irony in one of the world's most authoritarian and control-minded regimes seeing the rapid emergence of some of the world's most open organizations.

As entrepreneurs continue to experiment with new ideas, and to compete around the world, they will also increasingly place demands on the government. The government will have to meet those demands to keep the economy expanding and realize its development goals. There will inevitably be trade-offs between growth and control. We have already seen that government leaders and China's new entrepreneurs are conscious of those trade-offs, and so while the debate over control will undoubtedly continue, head-to-head public contests are unlikely.

RICHER—AND MORE RELAXED

During the remainder of Xi Jinping's presidency—due to run until 2023—we will see the emergence not just of a richer and more powerful China, but also a more confident, relaxed China. For now, Xi wants to take no risks, largely because of China's growth outlook, which will remain weak while the next round of economic reforms are carried out. For the country's leaders, who have made their ability to keep the economy developing their primary claim to legitimacy, this is a dangerous period.

Through this period, however, entrepreneurs will continue to drive their companies forward. I don't expect them to bargain with the government over their political needs, but I do expect them to constantly negotiate with the government, pointing out where they would like to see change and offering assurances of support in return.

The government will often find itself having to choose between protecting less-efficient state enterprises or allowing them to be displaced by more efficient private ones. In some circumstances, the government will support state firms; in others, it will allow the private ones to win. But overall, the private sector will expand to claim an ever greater share of almost every sector. This will result in a major shift in China's institutional makeup. Not only will private companies account for an even greater share of the economy than they now do, but the business playing field will grow increasingly level.

Many of the Yabuli forum entrepreneurs sense these changes. They are old enough to have lived through China's entire reform period. They have seen enormous changes unfold before their eyes as the country switched from central planning to embracing market forces.

Not only have they seen just what is possible in the transformation China has undergone in the last three decades, but they also can see that further changes are inevitable. They are aware of the role they and others in China's private sector have played in these changes. They do not claim total responsibility: they know that their achievements were not realized in a vacuum, and that to do what they have done required a very specific environment, one where the government liberalized sectors, allowed foreign investment, encouraged trade, and built infrastructure.

They also know that, while much of their leverage is indirect, without them what has happened in China would not have been possible. They are aware that the businesses they have created are powerful and that they have unleashed new forces in China that are changing many things—some directly, many more indirectly.

But they also are a little fearful that the achievements of the last three decades could be undone. Political will launched China's economic reforms, and while it is all but impossible to envision a political will that could reverse them, a lack of political will to continue with reforms is readily conceivable. Mechanisms to protect the achievements of China's entrepreneurs remain weak. Even without any reversal of economic reforms, much of their work could be undone by predatory officials placed in key local or national positions. This explains the emphasis that Victor Wang and other entrepreneurs place on moving China toward having the rule of law.

It is apparent that the government stands at a crossroads. Can it continue with the hybrid model—government control and economic liberalization—that has brought it so much success? Or must it reform further?

In many important respects, it does not have much choice. Short of trying to rewind China back to the 1970s, what China's private sector has created over the last three decades cannot be pushed away or held back. The economic and political consequences would be too great. Increasingly, moreover, the government has shown that it is aware of the needs and priorities of Chinese entrepreneurs.

Xi Jinping appears to have recognized this. Since assuming office, alongside his advocacy of a greater role for market forces, Xi's administration has also clamped down on all sources of dissent, including paying much closer attention to many NGOs, especially those pushing for legal reforms. The main motive for these actions, however, appears to lie in government fears about the impact of a slowing economy as officials wean the country off the debt-fueled model that saw it through the aftermath of the global financial crisis.

This suggests that while Xi's biggest challenge is ensuring China can make the transition to its next stage of economic development, his biggest fear is that a sharp reduction in growth might trigger social unrest. Add the fact that much of the underlying discontent that fueled the 1989 student-led democracy movement was caused by unhappiness over a big increase in corruption, and it's clear why Xi has also mounted a broader, deeper, and longer anticorruption campaign than any other in recent years.

In short, Xi is serious about economic reform, but also knows about the risks such reform brings with it. He wants to make sure his program is not thrown off course either by social unrest stemming from its short-term costs or by political opposition from vested interests who may see their access to power and wealth eroded. He and other party leaders also seem to be aware of the need to build up their own capabilities: to broaden and deepen their capacity to oversee a society that as well as becoming more prosperous is also becoming more diverse.

However, while Xi's clampdown on dissent and his anticorruption campaign have received widespread media coverage outside China, outspoken voices outside the arena of politics have not been silenced. As we have seen, Jack Ma and several other leading entrepreneurs are among the most vehement advocates of China's need to address its appalling environmental problems. Others, including Huang Nubo, continue to call for greater attention to be paid to meeting the social challenges created by development, especially the destruction of cultural practices caused by urbanization. And still others, especially figures from the Gang of '92 such as Chen Dongsheng and Victor Wang, push for a broader agenda of gradual reform through the

China Entrepreneurs Forum, especially for a greater role for the rule of law.

The China in which these people live is one that continues to be intolerant of even the slightest form of political dissent. It is not, however, a country that stifles all differences of opinion. Rather, it is a place that is increasingly looking for organizations beyond the state, including private companies, to provide the additional means necessary to solve the country's problems. The government wants wealth management companies to put pressure on the state-owned banks to improve their lending practices, private health-care companies to extend the range and quality of medical services, and Internet video providers to offer entertainment and information that contribute to people's well-being. Victor Wang and the other entrepreneurs who feel compelled to express their views on the direction of China's development are essentially pointing out that the new China that is emerging will be a more complex place than the one that existed just a couple of decades ago. They played a key role in creating this new China; they have ideas on how it can be managed, and are willing to contribute.

They know the impact they have had is enormous—reworking shopping, finance, communications, and a host of other industries, and in the process also transforming much of China's social fabric. They know what they are doing is changing the balance of forces in China and that this will be both accepted and resisted. And when they look to the future, they wonder whether it is possible to build on their business achievements and drive change in other areas. Someone as established as Jack Ma, for example, knows he can use his stature to call for a rethink of how China treats its environment (words he is backing up with

Changing China

action: in April 2014, Alibaba launched a campaign to map water quality across China, supplying testing kits that sent back results from users' smartphones).

We cannot know just how delicately the various contending forces are balanced. As Victor Wang made clear in his speech, many of China's entrepreneurs, especially those who founded their businesses in the 1980s and 1990s, are very much aware of how much change they have driven already in Chinese society at large. These were, after all, the people who seized the opportunities that sprung up in the 1990s to establish and build businesses, creating an entrepreneurial China that provided a springboard for subsequent generations of entrepreneurs. A question for many of them now is not just what changes may arise as a consequence of their business activities, but whether they can or should play a role in shaping future changes.

While many entrepreneurs would like to see the rule of law play a far greater role in China, for private property to have far greater protection, and to be subject to far less arbitrary interference from officials, so far, few have used their wealth to promote an overtly political agenda. Among the handful who have is Wang Gongquan, a venture capitalist who, after making a fortune from technology and real estate investments, began publicly advocating for China to develop a genuine civil society supported by a legal system operating independently of the government. He launched a civic group called the New Citizens Movement and built a following of more than 1.5 million people for his Sina Weibo account. Until 2013, the government warily tolerated most such organizations. Xi Jinping's assumption of the presidency changed that. Soon after he took office, in the same crackdown on dissent that led to Charles Xue's arrest, Wang was also detained.

Unsurprisingly, with examples like this before them, most entrepreneurs avoid any explicit involvement in politics. Liu Chuanzhi, the honorary chairman and former CEO of Lenovo, and another prominent member of the CEF, has long maintained a public stance of "no politics." But like Victor Wang, he also suggests that China needs to support and protect the country's main wealth creators, which in turn will require more than just economic changes. Speaking at a China Entrepreneurs Forum meeting in 2013, he told CNBC, "My view is that the Chinese government should adopt a more systematic and comprehensive approach when it comes to reform. For example, how to establish a better rule of law in this country so as to increase the creditworthiness of the government, so that the public will have more confidence and ensure a culture of mutual trust and honesty can be established. . . . That way the government can push through more social and political reforms that can be the basis of further economic reforms."

Will the government listen to voices such as those of Liu and Victor Wang? Almost certainly it already has. As the economy becomes ever more the preserve of the private sector, China's leaders will have to pay more attention to the needs of the country's entrepreneurs, and so communication channels such as the China Entrepreneurs Forum will grow in importance.

Those leaders accept that China is changing, and that the forces driving that change are not ones that they can directly control or whose outcome is predictable. But they are also leaders with a strong collective memory, who believe that China's reemergence stems principally from a steadfast commitment to social and political stability, which in turn calls for zero tolerance of any questioning of their right to rule. China's entrepreneurs may be changing China, but they are not the people who are running the country. They know this, and will not overstep their position. Wang Jianlin, the CEO of Dalian Wanda and one of China's richest individuals, has put it succinctly: "Be close to government, but far from politics."

6

THE RIGHT RESPONSE

"I 'm not talented. I started as a yokel with no choice but to learn," says Xu Lianjie with a chuckle. Xu is the CEO of Hengan International, China's leading manufacturer of sanitary napkins and disposable diapers. Though it is a $2.7 billion company, it has been headquartered since its founding in his hometown, Jinjiang, a small coastal city in Fujian Province, about midway between Shanghai and Hong Kong.

Despite operating out of this remote location, Xu—like Ren Zhengfei at Huawei, Zhang Ruimin at Haier, Li Shufu at Geely, and other of China's leading entrepreneurs—has built a business centered on taking full benefit of the advantages and demands of China's market scale and rate of change. Like his peers, he is also throwing down a major challenge to foreign competitors, especially the world's leading fast-moving consumer-goods firms such as Procter & Gamble, Kimberly-Clark, Johnson & Johnson, and Japan's Kao.

The Right Response

With a weather-beaten face, Xu still looks like the farmer he was when he founded his company back in 1985. Like many Chinese entrepreneurs who started out in the early years of China's reform era, he began with little knowledge of business: "I was a farmer with no culture," he says. "I didn't even graduate from elementary school. I had no understanding of management; I couldn't read financial statements." Nonetheless, in three decades he has built Hengan into a company with rapid growth and global aspirations. Its revenues have doubled in the past four years, and it maintains a nearly 20 percent profit margin, despite increasing competition in China from Japanese, American, and other Chinese companies.

When Xu set up Hengan in 1985 with Sze Man Bok, now the company's chairman, most of the businesses in Jinjiang were small-scale garment factories making unbranded clothing and struggling to get by. But Deng Xiaoping's economic reforms, launched barely half a decade earlier, were already raising living standards. Xu saw that his neighbors had more money to spend and were looking for products that brought greater convenience and comfort to their lives. Casting around for a product that would meet such needs, he decided to enter China's nascent market for sanitary napkins. Instead of importing raw materials, as most other manufacturers did, he invested in building his own paper plant. This pushed costs up, but Xu's hunch that higher quality would lead to customer loyalty proved correct. Within a couple of years, Hengan displaced the other local sanitary-napkin manufacturers, most of them state-owned, in Fujian and other nearby coastal provinces and cities.

Starting in the late 1980s, however, Hengan found itself facing a very different kind of competitor—multinational companies, led by Procter & Gamble. Xu and Sze responded by expanding production and continuing to raise the quality of Hengan's products. They bought more equipment from overseas, began to invest heavily in brand building, and, perhaps most important, built up in-house teams of sales staff, sending them out across the country.

Today, numbering more than 15,000 people, these "feet on the street" ensure that Hengan's products are available in more than 800,000 stores nationwide. With its multinational rivals relying on wholesalers to distribute their goods, Hengan has been able both to grow faster and to expand its product range. The most important of these additions were tissues, which now account for nearly half of Hengan's revenue thanks to its 20 percent share of China's market, and disposable diapers.

The one blip in the company's progress came in the mid 1990s when management bottlenecks in production and distribution led to sales stalling. This was an unintended consequence of the company's recruiting practices; in its early years, many of its shareholders and executives had been relatives and family friends of the founders, and they lacked the skills and background needed to run and oversee what had become a large business.

Xu realized he needed to professionalize Hengan's operations. To move the company to the next level, Hengan was floated on the Hong Kong Stock Exchange in 1998. Much of the money raised was used to reorganize and rationalize the company's ownership and governance structure, buying out many of its original shareholders and replacing most of its executives with professional managers.

Xu then turned to the outside world for help with his next step, paying $2.5 million to an American consultancy, Thomas Group, to come up with a blueprint to restructure Hengan. As part of his strategy to keep standards rising and the company's organization aligned with its growth, he has repeated this measure several times (I worked with him on a consulting project with Booz & Company in 2007). Most recently, in 2013, he hired IBM to overhaul Hengan's supply-chain and information-technology systems, two elements that will play a crucial part in his plans to more than double revenues again in the next few years.

Xu is now broadening Hengan's product range to include foods and snacks. Like many other of China's most successful entrepreneurs, he is also leading Hengan in its first steps abroad. So far, overseas revenues are negligible, accounting for just 5 percent of Hengan's revenues and all earned in other emerging markets in Asia. But with China's own growth slowing, he is searching for other countries similar to China where he can apply Hengan's experience and exploit the advantages of its domestically developed economies of scale.

LAYING DOWN A CHALLENGE

In many of China's liberalized markets, including appliances, televisions, motorcycles, and telecom equipment, Chinese manufacturers have already successfully challenged foreign manufacturers. In others, such as computers, many fast-moving consumer goods, industrial equipment, auto components, and medical equipment, private Chinese companies such as Hengan, Sany, Mindray, Wanxiang, and Lenovo have established themselves as major competitors to international firms in China and in some cases overseas. These businesses have not based their success on just producing cheaper versions of international products—though that has been an important tactic for almost all of them—but on committing to improve their products and their processes continuously. They use Chinese strengths *and* bring in Western expertise to refine their operations. They focus on developing scale for the Chinese market while also ensuring that their structures have the flexibility necessary to change as that market expands and transforms itself. And, almost without exception, they are intent on being the best in their sector. Each of their owners knows that one company will have to be the best in its industry, and each wants to be the leader.

If multinational companies are to respond effectively to these Chinese competitors, they will have to take into account the broad front across which China's leading entrepreneurial companies are competing. This means not simply thinking about price, or selling into lower-tier markets, or producing clones or copies of goods developed elsewhere. Rather, it is about developing businesses that are fit to compete in China—with the entire range of capabilities needed to thrive in its complex, fast-changing markets—and then taking those businesses to other markets, including their home one, overseas.

Although many multinationals have been operating in China for 20 years, and in some cases longer, most of them have yet to take on board the nature of the challenge they face. Looking back over the past two decades, it is possible to pick out some notable success stories. Carmakers Volkswagen and GM, despite rules forcing them to work in 50-50 joint ventures as as part of government efforts to develop an indigenous state-owned car industry, have both built giant auto firms in which they call the shots. Yum!

Brands' KFC restaurants, likewise, have been the runaway success in their sector, far outperforming global rival McDonald's. Luxury brands of almost every nature have proved hugely popular with China's acutely status-conscious middle class.

Of course, there have been some notable failures. Home Depot arrived in China expecting to sell its DIY products to the country's new homeowning class, only to find that the last thing the proud owners of a new apartment wanted to do was decorate their own flat. Similarly, UK supermarket chain Tesco spent more than $2 billion trying—and failing—to secure enough customers over nine years before handing its stores over in 2013 to state-owned China Resources Enterprise, the country's biggest retailer.

But far more common than the members of either of these categories are the ones in between—the hundreds of thousands of companies that have poured into China but have never quite been able to declare their operations a major success. Take Pepsi, which struggled for years to build a business in China before eventually selling its bottling business to the Taiwan beverage and packaged-food company Tingyi. Similarly, Nissan's Infiniti and Toyota's Lexus both badly lag their German luxury counterparts such as BMW, Volkswagen's Audi, and Daimler's Mercedes-Benz.

The majority of foreign-owned companies are not ready for what is coming next. They know that China is strategically unavoidable. They know that China is already the world's biggest market for many goods. They know that China is becoming the source of new competitive advantages, from the new products and processes emerging from its companies and research institutions to its huge economies of scale, which companies can use to enhance their businesses in other parts of the world. They know they cannot afford to miss the opportunity to build their presence in China as a means of competing against the new Chinese entrants to their global industries. But they are not sure how to react.

Some of this indecision can be attributed to China's operating environment becoming tougher. Costs are rising across the board for everything from land and labor to marketing and advertising. The government has removed some of the privileges used to attract foreign capital through the 1990s and 2000s, such as tax breaks and preferential access to investment zones. President Xi Jinping's drive to introduce further economic reforms may be aimed at allowing market forces to have a greater role in disciplining the economy, but liberalization of markets to further overseas investment will continue to be gradual, continuing the pattern laid down some 20 years ago.

In the first half of 2014, both U.S. and European investment into China appeared to be catching its breath, down around 5 percent over the same period the previous year. Japan's investment fell nearly 50 percent, largely as a result of its ongoing dispute with China over the ownership of islands it calls Senkaku and China knows as Diaoyu in the East China Sea. Foreign companies are also starting to complain more about unfair treatment. Many of them are becoming nervous that the great promise of China's huge population, into which they have committed trillions of dollars, may prove just beyond their grasp. They are worried that operating in China may prove too difficult: its fast-changing markets too complex for them to master, its local firms too powerful and well endowed with local knowledge, and its government too protective of domestic interests.

The Right Response

COMPETING ON THE EDGE

Writing about the fast-changing computing and information-technology industries of the 1990s, Shona L. Brown, a consultant and ex–Google executive, and Kathleen M. Eisenhardt, a professor at Stanford University, coined the phrase "competing on the edge." That phrase, and much of the behavior associated with it, can be applied to China's business environment of today. Brown and Eisenhardt saw the information and communication technology industries of the 1990s as occupying an intermediate state between order and chaos, with change occurring in unprecedented and unpredictable ways, boundaries between previously separate industries erased, and hypercompetition leading to the fast rise and fall of companies. They argued that under these conditions, business strategy had three principal characteristics.

First, advantage can only be temporary. For companies to succeed, they must continuously generate new sources of advantage. Change, rather than being viewed as a threat to their existing business, should instead be treated as the key source of new opportunities for growth.

Second, as a result of advantage being temporary, strategy will have to be diverse and emergent, and defy simple generalization. Companies must always consider a broad array of options, with resulting actions likely to involve a diverse collection of loosely linked moves whose overall direction is at best only semi-coherent. Goals and plans will always be shifting in accordance with the opportunities and constraints of the business environment.

And third, reinvention will lie at the heart of all of a company's activities. In its constant search for new ways to create value, innovation of processes as well as products will be crucial, meaning that organizations will have to constantly change how they operate as well as what they make. Efficiency will count for less than the ability to generate and test new ideas, though companies will also have to make sure they don't waste resources, especially because reliable long-term sources of profit will be rare.

In an environment of hyper-competition and change, companies can never settle into a stable equilibrium. At the same time, however, they should be aware of the dangers of being too fixated on the future. Indeed, Brown and Eisenhardt suggest they should avoid envisioning a future and then trying to move toward that vision, but rather remain rooted in the present, making sure they gain maximum benefit from their existing products by extending offerings to new market segments and developing and exploiting derivative products. Brown and Eisenhardt call this process "stretching out the past." They argue that companies should use their existing strengths to launch experimental products and services to test the market or move into new business areas while paying enough attention to their existing business and its ability to generate the resources necessary to support new products and directions.

Almost all of China's leading entrepreneurial companies exemplify these three trends. Because China's markets are at multiple stages of development, they know that while in one market a product may soon need to have its features overhauled and upgraded as consumers there become richer, there are certainly other markets the product should be "stretched" to. Haier, for example, has constantly found new niches for its products by adding features—making washing machines that could rinse vegetables, aimed at rural markets, or shrinking its fridges to make them appeal to students living in cramped accommodations. Huawei and Lenovo operate similarly, constantly iterating and launching new models of their smartphones, tablets, and other products.

All these companies want to be around for the long haul, but they also know that tests and products must be aimed at the immediate future because the period beyond that is unknowable. Alibaba continues to jump into new areas of business where its current capabilities have to be extended. Examples include adapting the model of its B2B business, Alibaba.com, to create the C2C enterprise Taobao; bringing together its business and consumer models from Alibaba.com and Taobao to launch Tmall; using the knowledge of its business customers to start a business lending money to small companies; and moving into consumer finance with Alipay.

Given the rate of market change, companies have to set a rhythm and tempo around the number of new products and services they offer, refreshing and launching them in accordance with the tempo and rhythm of the market. They must pay close attention to the order and timing in which they do things. While moving too slowly will almost inevitably mean allowing a competitor to steal a march, moving too fast can also create problems, especially if a market has yet to reach the right stage of development for a product or service.

In terms of organization, to guard against being locked into outdated competitive models, businesses must continuously realign how they operate and what they produce with emerging opportunities. They need just enough structure to keep things from flying apart. Since success will come from being able to move nimbly and fast, strategy cannot be driven from the top down. Instead, it should be driven from the business unit level up.

All these companies combine reiteration and reinvention. Tencent has moved from computer-based messaging to online games and then to mobile messaging. But WeChat's roots also clearly extend back to its original hit, the QQ instant-messaging program; its stream of new features taps into the need for constant iteration to keep consumers in search of novelty happy. The giveaway model with paid-for add-ons, developed for QQ, was extended to online games; that same model, complete with games, is now a core part of Tencent's mobile strategy.

Overall, the outcome is that strategy is diverse—obviously so at Alibaba and Tencent, but also at businesses such as Geely, where Li Shufu is simultaneously maintaining the separation between Volvo's global and Chinese businesses, keeping a gap between those two businesses and his Geely operations, and preparing for a possibly very different future with his electric-vehicle acquisitions. This approach is well described by Haier's CEO, Zhang Ruimin: "The CEO of a company should seek balance between systems, rules, and chaos. On the one hand, he should change with the world. But on the other, he should avoid chaotic changes and build an inner rule of changing."

BETWEEN RULES AND CHAOS

Brown and Eisenhardt proposed their model as a strategy for companies in the United States. But it is even more applicable to China, where most leading entrepreneurial companies already behave in the manner they described as appropriate for that environment.

Using Brown and Eisenhardt's insights, multinational companies should revisit the forces that are shaping the Chinese business environment: its market opening, the role officials play in shaping and supporting growth, and the impact of technology, especially the Internet.

In Chapter 2, I highlighted how this trio of factors has contributed to growth, creating a hypercompetitive business environment characterized by lowering barriers between many industries. With few companies having reliable sources of long-term profits, Chinese businesses are forced to become agile and nimble, able to transform themselves and seize opportunities, even outside their own fields of expertise.

In developed countries, similar trends can be seen in industries touched by the Internet and digitization, with music, the media, and publishing being turned on their heads, to name just three. But across many industries the Internet hasn't fundamentally changed which kind of companies remain on top. Banks and financial companies still dominate finance, automotive companies remain carmakers, energy companies are still energy companies.

In China, however, the overall impact has been far greater. Increasingly driven by the rise of the mobile Internet, we not only see online businesses jumping into finance, logistics, and the media, but delivery companies jumping into retailing and e-commerce; battery companies jumping into carmaking; appliance makers reinventing themselves as Internet businesses; and computing, telecom-equipment, and start-up firms all leaping into smartphones, to name just a few.

These abrupt jumps in new directions can be attributed to two things: the still underdeveloped nature of China's markets due to many industries having been created from scratch in just a few years; and the rate of market change, which creates difficulties for even the most successful companies in establishing any kind of long-term sustainable advantage. Companies have to react to events continually, changing their products and product mix, moving into new regions, testing new lines of business. Even a company such as Haier, which would seem to be strongly positioned in the white goods industry, feels insecure.

The most successful companies are those that can keep evolving, expanding their business into new areas, building scale, and fending off competition. They are the ones that keep modifying and adapting their products to take account of changes in China's markets, keeping just ahead of their competitors.

Translating the abstract notions of Brown and Eisenhardt into concrete strategies for China is a challenge. Clearly, there is no one-size-fits-all answer to the question of just how much of an international company's business should be China-based. Nonetheless, the fundamental challenge for multinationals today, faced with the rise of Chinese entrepreneurial companies, is to reassess the potential China offers them to maintain their long-term viability.

To do this, they need to turn conventional thinking on its head. Traditionally, multinationals have seen the hardest part of putting a global strategy together as how to scale across regions— taking products and operational strengths that have brought them success in one or two regions and then applying them in other markets around the world. What they need to do in China is the opposite: figure out how best to configure their operations there and then use their China-developed strengths to improve their performance in the rest of the world.

The Right Response

KNOW CHINA AND ITS CONTEXT

China will be the place where companies develop the "competing-on-the-edge" skills they need to thrive in the next decade and beyond—not simply because of the size of its market, but because of the combination of that size with its rate of change.

As we have seen, many international companies entered China in the last two decades without first preparing for a long-term commitment. They set up operations to test the water, rotated expat managers in and out of the country, and periodically flew in their CEO to shake hands with officials. A lot of them went on to develop successful sourcing and export operations, tapping into the sourcing networks that rapidly built up around the Pearl River delta in Guangdong, the Yangtze river delta around Shanghai, and at several other locations.

But when it came to selling into China's markets, many struggled. Despite their global experience, financial strength, and technological advantages, many were surprised when strategies tested and tried in other parts of the world failed in China. Some were ambushed by local firms. Others were justifiably upset when their partners took their technology and started separate businesses of their own, making a similar or in some cases identical product. Many struggled to cope with infrastructure shortcomings, talent shortages, fickle customers, and lower-priced local alternatives to their products.

For most of these companies, the reason why they struggled was simply that they entered China knowing too little about its context—the complexities of its history, culture, geography, and politics. Such ignorance can no longer be excused. To be competitive in China, the first step any international company must take is to get to know China as thoroughly as possible.

Acquiring and absorbing this kind of knowledge takes time, and companies will have to develop ways of both acquiring and retaining knowledge about China. China can no longer be the kind of place that executives are rotated in and out of. Indeed, the single most important step a company can take in this direction is to develop a truly locally committed team.

With a deep understanding of China in place, a company can then set about understanding what capabilities it will need to succeed. Most multinationals have developed clear and strong global functional capabilities and believe they are able to operate their business in more or less the same way in many parts of the world. Expecting China to be similar, they tend to cut-and-paste their strategies and business models. Sometimes this works, but more often it leads to frustration and friction between in-country executives, who can see all too clearly that the old models aren't working, and managers of global functions, often proud of their achievements and status, who continue to believe the same standards and processes should be applied around the world.

The realities of China call for the opposite of this approach. Rather than deciding which parts of their global operating model can be leveraged for China, they should consider what capabilities will have to be developed in China for China. Getting the balance right between the two will require a deep reflection on changes in process, in decision rights, in key performance indicators, and especially in mind-set and culture.

For most companies, the biggest of these mind-set changes will be accepting that China's rate of evolution will call for constantly having to rework strategies and practices. As China continues to evolve in a fast and often discontinuous manner, managers in multinational companies will need to know how to anticipate, capture, and handle opportunities and threats. According to Shane Tedjarati, Honeywell's Shanghai-based president of Global High-Growth Regions, "You don't become Chinese, but you become a competitor to the Chinese. That means you need to understand how they compete and importantly how they think."

The best method of coping in this environment will be to adopt Chinese ways: studying the strategies Chinese companies use to overcome the obstacles they face and adopting similarly flexible and resourceful methods and processes, especially in the areas of decision-making, corporate flexibility, and innovations.

★ **Accelerate decision-making.** As success in China will depend on acting fast whenever a potentially rich opportunity is found, decisions must be taken quickly and locally. Speed of reaction will be vital to take advantage of possible opportunities for fast growth in an emerging market for a new product or service. Headquarters will also have to grant their China operations substantial autonomy. As mistakes will be inevitable, headquarters will also have to tolerate a high degree of risk and experimentation, allowing their China arms to test new business areas and acquire new capabilities in the same way as local firms, possibly extending into areas that their parent company might feel uncomfortable about entering in other parts of the world. Should, for example, a company offer a stripped-down, cheaper version of one of its products if doing so risks cannibalizing sales of its other products elsewhere? Answers to such questions will seldom be black-and-white, but resolving them will call for addressing issues such as whether growth in China could result in scale for a product that could then be taken overseas, or whether other Chinese companies are producing a similar good that could undermine the international company's more advanced products. Either way, a company will have to move fast. Delays caused by waiting for approvals up and down the ladder will let many opportunities disappear.

★ **Increase flexibility.** Chinese conditions vary and change so rapidly that companies based there have to bring a great deal of flexibility to their operations and decision-making. They have to overcome logistic and supply-chain barriers in areas where transportation, communication, and financial infrastructure are weak—and then see barriers to entry come down when infrastructure conditions improve. For example, many Chinese companies routinely adopt ideas developed elsewhere for their own businesses and markets, making them their own in the process. As we have seen, Alibaba, Tencent, Baidu, and Meituan all used American-developed business models as inspiration for their own businesses, but then transformed them by adding features appropriate for Chinese users.

Before long we should also see the flow going the other way, with American Internet companies such as Twitter or Facebook-owned WhatsApp taking inspiration from the best ideas of Chinese companies such as Sina Weibo or Tencent's WeChat. Foreign companies can also learn from the way in which Chinese companies focus on their customers, constantly updating and modifying their products to keep pace with changes in needs and tastes. Xiaomi's engagement with its users is exemplary in this respect not just because it listens to what they say, but because of the way it acts immediately on the feedback it receives.

★ **Innovate the Chinese way.** When it comes to innovation, foreign companies can study how local enterprises constantly update and augment their products and capabilities, making them capable of penetrating and taking over entire high-technology sectors from the bottom up, as Huawei has done.

For products, this can be done the traditional way: filling R&D departments with locally hired science and engineering graduates, then putting them to work developing new goods and updating older ones to keep them in line with the fast-changing vagaries of local demand. Some companies are already taking this route. There are currently more than 1,300 R&D centers established by multinationals in China. Among them are GE, which has used ultralow-cost medical equipment developed in China to succeed in the country, and Dutch electronics firm Philips, which has made China its global center for LED lamp research.

Perhaps a more fruitful approach will be to come up with answers aimed at overcoming China's operational headaches. At most multinationals, innovation is principally directed at new products and technologies; in China, it is principally directed at coming up with multiple responses to allow a company to overcome the problems it faces on almost every front. When Alibaba rolled out Alipay, it had to overcome China's financial infrastructure shortcomings—the lack of an online payments system—and its regulatory limits, which made no provision for establishing an electronic payment system independent of its banks. While foreign companies are advised not to take too many risks with regulators in China, that should not prevent them from considering innovative solutions to operational challenges, and stretching their business to new areas if that helps them get ahead.

The potential of in-China innovation is not restricted to Chinese companies. A decade ago, industrial conglomerate Honeywell had minimal business in China. Today, China is its second-largest source of revenue after the United States, with growth continuing at more than 20 percent annually. This growth stems almost entirely from sales of China-developed control systems and other products developed specifically for the local market at R&D centers in Shanghai, Beijing, Tianjin, Nanjing, and Chongqing. Staffed with more than 1,400 scientists and engineers, Honeywell has invested more than half a billion dollars across these facilities since 2010.

FIND THE RIGHT PARTNERS

In the 1990s, Sino-foreign joint ventures were the Chinese government's preferred business structure for overseas investors, when it was eager to see as much technology transferred to local companies as possible. In the 2000s, joint ventures fell out of fashion, to be replaced by wholly foreign-owned enterprises, as multinationals wanted greater control over their own China operations. Now, once again, finding the right partner to work with is the best way of building a strong presence in China for many firms.

Whereas in the 1990s that meant finding the right joint-venture partner, now it can mean finding partners in many different areas. At its most straightforward, this could involve nothing more than taking an equity stake. If done early enough, the returns can be spectacular; witness the 34 percent of Tencent bought by South African media group Naspers in 2001, or the stakes held in Alibaba by Softbank (32 percent) and Yahoo (22.6 percent stake). Yihaodian is also majority foreign-owned since Wal-Mart raised its stake to 51 percent in 2012.

Local acquisitions and taking over established domestic brands are key ways of reaching deeper into China. In September 2014, for example, chocolate maker Hershey committed $577 million to buy Golden Monkey, a privately owned Shanghai-based candy maker, announcing that China was its number-one priority market outside the United States. Other companies following this route are the UK's Reckitt Benckiser, with its acquisition of Guilong Pharmaceutical, one of the country's leading makers of traditional Chinese medicine, and Switzerland's Nestlé, with a string of local purchases, among them Yinlu, China's tenth-largest soft drinks maker.

Another method for developing partners is to find a Chinese company that can take a foreign product to Chinese customers. Shanghai-based conglomerate Fosun bought a stake of just under 10 percent of Club Med for 46 million euros in 2010. Six months later, it had helped Club Med open its first resort in China. Plans for more to follow look certain to be implemented after Fosun bought control of Club Med in early 2015.

In 2013, Hertz Global Rental took a 20 percent stake in China's biggest car-rental firm, privately owned China Auto Rental. Overnight, the U.S. company's presence in China expanded from

5 outlets to 700. China Auto Rental got access to Hertz's customer referrals, one of the main sources of business for car rentals. This sector will only grow in importance as China's car-rental market grows from $4 billion to $20 billion—equaling America's.

Even more simply, as most consumer e-commerce in China is done through marketplaces rather than through company Web sites, a company could simply sell through Alibaba's Tmall. Among the many brands with stores on the site are Adidas, Nike, Marks and Spencer, Levi's, and Forever 21.

Doing so both avoids the hassles in setting up and running a freestanding e-commerce site, and in some cases, even the licensing necessary to sell goods in the country. Indeed, since Alibaba launched Tmall Global at the start of 2014, with a range of support services including a direct delivery service to addresses in the country, even companies with no Chinese presence can sell through the site.

MAKE LOCAL LEADERSHIP YOUR NUMBER-ONE PRIORITY

Finally, multinational companies must focus on the quality of their executives in China, both expatriate and Chinese. These people must understand and internalize the China context, acquire the skills and experience to build and instill the critical institutional knowledge for doing business in China, and ensure a high degree of alignment between China's realities and the expectations of global headquarters. Indeed, ensuring that headquarters understands both the constraints of operating in China as well as the potential opportunities it presents is one of the single most important factors determining whether a multinational company can succeed in China. Expectations for a company's China business are often overly optimistic or pessimistic over a very short time horizon, making decisions erratic.

Obviously, running a fully integrated China business is no longer a task that can be handled by a team from outside the country. The great majority of foreign companies in China today understand the importance of recruiting and developing Chinese staff up to the very highest levels. But localization or building local leadership means not only hiring and developing a few senior Chinese executives. It means developing the right mind-set and culture and a purpose that can resonate with the entire team. Indeed, whether the local leader is Chinese or not is less important than whether he or she has the leadership ability, mind-set, cultural affinity, and willingness to learn and adapt that are needed to create an organization flexible enough for China.

Among those who have stood out in the last decade are Yum! Brands' Sam Su, General Mills' Gary Chu, and Tetra Pak's Hudson Lee, all of whom are ethnic Chinese. But just as successful have been non-Chinese nationals Aditya Sehgal at Reckitt Benckiser, Shane Tedjarati at Honeywell, Roland Decorvet at Nestlé, and Roland Gerke at Bosch Siemens. What this quartet have in common is they all went to China and stayed there, acquiring both an extraordinarily rich understanding of the nuances of doing business in the country and the ability to share that understanding with the highest levels of their respective companies.

In parallel, some Chinese entrepreneurial firms have become major magnets for international talent. For instance, several of

China's leading Internet companies have a substantial number of foreign executives or local people with rich foreign experience working for them. As mentioned before, Jack Ma's right-hand person at Alibaba has long been Joe Tsai, who was born in Taiwan and educated in the United States. Tencent's Pony Ma has surrounded himself with foreign and Chinese executives with deep global experience. Both Mas have used these hires to gain access to international funding and expertise. Lei Jun at Xiaomi similarly brought in Google's Hugo Barra to guide his company's move into international markets.

The challenge for international companies will be to keep up. Can their efforts at integrating Chinese-style practices keep pace with the rate at which Chinese companies will add international capabilities?

TAKE YOUR CHINA STRENGTHS TO THE WORLD

As I mentioned above, many multinational companies continue to view China as an offshoot of their global operations. Instead, they should ask themselves whether their China business should be part of the foundations of their entire business. Is it possible, for example, to use capabilities developed in China not only to succeed in China but to enhance performance globally? Indeed, could companies plausibly apply advantages acquired in China to their global operations in a way that results in China becoming *the* core part of their global strategy? The answer isn't necessarily yes (though it could be "not yet"). Because of the size, speed, and complexity of the China market, demand patterns in different sectors are typically far more complicated and diverse than in other markets around the world. Often companies find that they need to pursue a larger-than-expected number of market segments if they want to sell their products throughout China.

In addition, boundaries of industries are often being redefined due to the emergence of new technologies, with the rise of wireless Internet being probably the most influential of recent advances.

The combination of a complicated and quickly changing demand pattern, hypercompetition, reworked industry boundaries, and discontinuities in the regulatory context requires companies, both foreign and Chinese, to develop new sources of competitive advantage in order to secure a better market position. These new sources of competitive advantage can manifest in various ways—new products, technologies, brands, ways to go to market, service models, and even entire business models.

Foreign companies will find themselves compelled to integrate the advantages that China-based operations have into their global value chains—developing products there, selling into its markets, and then using the economies of scale China allows to take those goods to the rest of the world. Chinese companies are already doing this: driven by the hunger and ambition of their owners, many want to take their products everywhere, especially to the world's developed markets.

Multinational companies should not view China as "another" market. If a company's China operations are not granted a central position in corporate strategizing, it is unlikely they will receive the resources and support to ensure their growth. To make China an integral part of their global businesses, most companies will have to adjust their organizations and give China-based executives far higher decision rights than they have enjoyed until now—not just in China, but over many other operations around the world. Such a change calls for a significant shift in corporate mind-set and culture, but it is one that must be made.

In summary, for many companies, China has the potential to become the world's leading breeding ground for growth and innovation. Being aware of this will be a crucial responsibility of executives not just in China but also at headquarters around the world.

HUMILITY NEEDED

China matters today both because of the wealth it has created in the last 15 years and its industrial development that now allows it to compete effectively on a global scale. One of the reasons it is richer is the emergence of successful Chinese entrepreneurial companies that collectively hire and pay hundreds of millions of people. As these companies become more successful, they make life harder for international companies. No longer are they hunting for sales just in lower-tier markets and regions, but, like Hengan, they are moving into middle- and even upper-tier markets, and seeking to expand further.

In China, international companies must come to terms with the fact that business has become tougher and more complex than ever before. Blaming the government, unfair competition, intellectual-property piracy, and so on is a distraction from the real reason: that more and more of China's entrepreneurial companies have reached the stage where they are viable competitors both at home and overseas.

To cope, international companies will have to acquire better knowledge of Chinese conditions; they will have to localize their operations, and develop local staff, as they will find Chinese companies competing more and more both in their areas of expertise and in their markets around the world, including their home turf.

This does not mean multinationals will have to become as Chinese as Chinese companies, but they must adopt and adapt the techniques of the most successful Chinese companies for their own purposes. While the rise of Chinese entrepreneurs will not result in a shift to a China-centered economy everywhere, it will force more companies to run themselves in a similar way to Chinese companies—operating more in the present, viewing themselves as in a condition of constant flux, and always searching for new business areas they can stretch themselves into.

Thirty years ago, Chinese companies had a lot to learn. Three decades of learning, however, have given them—and especially their longest-serving CEOs, figures such as Hengan's Xu Lianjie, Haier's Zhang Ruimin, and Huawei's Ren Zhengfei—much to share.

One of the most astute observations from these leaders is Zhang Ruimin's notion that, given the speed at which things change, companies can never declare themselves successful; the best they can hope for is that they are capable of moving with the times in which they find themselves. With China also continuing to change, its entrepreneurs have to be constantly reorganizing their operations, as Zhang Ruimin is doing once again at Haier, as

Pony Ma has done at Tencent in switching the focus from its QQ messaging system to online games and now to WeChat, and of course as Jack Ma has done repeatedly at Alibaba. International companies wondering how to react to the rise of China should study these and the other Chinese companies building what in a few years will be the world's biggest economy.

For multinationals, a similar humility is needed. Acknowledging this, and accepting that much has to be learned afresh, will play a crucial role in determining whether a multinational can be successful in China.

7

THE LAND OF
OPPORTUNITIES

Jessica Wong, 32, and Frank Yao, 30, started cosmetics brand Panda W in 2011. Graduates of prestigious universities in Beijing and Shanghai, they had both established careers at well-known and respected companies, Jessica with the French cosmetics business L'Oréal and Frank with China Merchants Bank, China's largest privately owned bank.

Both learned a lot working within these large organizations, but they were also frustrated. Both L'Oréal and China Merchants Bank were scrambling to keep up with China's extraordinary pace of growth. They sucked in thousands of young managers like Jessica and Frank, and accepted their ideas for growing the business. There was no way to stand out from the pack, and both of the young graduates felt like cogs in a great machine. Surely, reasoned Jessica and Frank, if all that growth was out there, couldn't they tap it too? They decided to venture out on their own.

They started by selling other companies' products, but quickly realized there were far better prospects in developing their own. They developed a mobile phone app: a "magic mirror" that, using a picture of someone's face, would recommend skin products and cosmetics. Though they initially licensed it to other companies as a sales channel, they saw potential for using this kind of marketing capability to develop their own brand of skin products.

Their first product was a facial mask to alleviate wrinkles. A designer friend from Taiwan came up with some packaging ideas. Another group of friends helped them develop the name Panda W and their cartoon panda bear logo. Using the cash generated by sales of other companies' goods, they promoted their brand through advertisements in fashion magazines. They kept other costs low by taking all their orders online through a store on Alibaba's Tmall, with payment taken through Alipay and goods dispatched across China by courier.

Three years later, their business is thriving. They have a staff of 20, all in their 20s or early 30s, working across two rooms of a start-up incubator not far from the center of Shanghai. They have extended their range of products to skin-care creams and added other online outlets including Jumei.com and Vipshop, China's two biggest cosmetic Web sites. (Jumei.com is well established enough to be listed on the New York Stock Exchange.)

They haven't become rich yet, and maybe they never will. According to Wong, China now has more than 30,000 cosmetic brands selling their goods through thousands of e-commerce outlets that crowd the Chinese Internet.

"Every day I'm worried," says Wong. "We face so many problems, it's like taking the *gaoko* every day," she adds, referring to China's notorious hypercompetitive college-entrance exam, which determines the future of millions of young people each year. Yet far more powerful than her fears—and more compelling than the possibility of earning a lot of money—are the autonomy and freedom that running a business brings. She and Yao are doing something that would have been inconceivable in China a few decades ago. It would have been hard to imagine even a tiny market of consumers for these products at all, let alone enabling their purchase through technologies like the Internet and smartphones. Most surprising of all is the fact that people like Wong and Yao, running online businesses, make a living while remaining largely off the official radar.

FEARS AND HOPES

The Panda W founders are relatively carefree, even though some might argue they have several reasons to be fearful for their future. First of all, failure is frequent for private companies in China, which are exposed to its hypercompetitive business environment. Some entrepreneurs, chiefly those from the generation who launched their businesses in the early 1990s, achieve rapid success that fades away even more quickly than it arrived.

Second, uncertainty is dangerous. Outside observers often miss how deeply this sense of danger is ingrained in the Chinese psyche, particularly for those in their 50s or older, who lived through the turmoil of the Cultural Revolution and the political shifts that followed. The extraordinary upheavals China has undergone in the past century should give pause to anyone who sees the country's current stability as permanent. Possibly it may endure, but given the country's recent history, can anyone be certain? Its rulers aren't—hence their preoccupation with maintaining public order.

Third, the pace of change leads to a sense of continual restlessness.

This explains some of the ambivalent views of success held by older Chinese entrepreneurs, such as Haier's Zhang Ruimin. They feel they can never rest, because there are always going to be new competitors, or new technologies, that threaten their secure position. Still, China's younger generations are full of hope. Like many older people in China, Jessica Wong's mother worries about China returning to the era of little or no social welfare, but Jessica doesn't. China's unemployment and health-care safety net may be weak, but it exists. Of course, Panda W could fail and Wong might have to find some other way of making a living, but she needn't worry about failure leading to starvation, a very real concern just a few decades ago. Nor need she worry about political persecution, as she would have had to before the late 1970s. Anyone born since the early 1980s has lived his or her entire life under conditions of extreme economic growth. For members of this generation, as for their parents, change is the norm, but now change is mostly positive. Cities have been transformed beyond all recognition, bicycles have been abandoned for cars, and malls have replaced street markets.

Having lived through this period of dizzying growth, younger entrepreneurs are far less worried about things going sour than many older entrepreneurs. Indeed, their outlook is almost the opposite. Whereas many older entrepreneurs went into business in order to gain some security, Wong likes running her own business because it allows her to establish her own area of freedom where she is in charge of her life. She and others her age embrace the wrenching changes China has gone through over the last three and a half decades. The country's social fabric may have been stretched and reworked, but life is more secure, more comfortable, and more interesting.

A DIFFERENT OUTLOOK

Notice how different the views of China's entrepreneurs are from the mainstream outlook on China held by most Western observers, who focus largely on the country's multiple problems: its pollution, ballooning debt, aging population, potential for social unrest, poor human rights records, and mistrust of democracy. Most Chinese people recognize these problems, but they see their country as a land of fast-growing opportunities.

The aspirations of the Chinese people are closely tied to China's reemergence as one of the world's leading economic powers. Once again, they hope, it can be a source of new ideas and inventions as good as, if not better than, those from anywhere else. As we've seen, the country's technological capability stands at the brink of a major leap forward, and many businesspeople in China recognize this and are preparing for it. The country's entrepreneurs, because of the nature of what they do, are best positioned to make technological change come true.

The state remains a powerful force, though its influence on people's lives is much more indirect than it used to be. In the mid 1990s, for example, most people in cities worked for state-owned enterprises; they lived in homes owned by those enterprises, did much of their shopping in state-owned stores, traveled on public transport, watched state-owned television channels, and even had their potential marriage partners vetted by local committees. Today, many Chinese citizens live in homes they own, work for private companies, shop online or in privately owned supermarkets, have their own cars, and watch entertainment from around the world via Youku or one of the other Internet video services. They are free to choose where to work, whom to date, when to marry, and where to travel on their holidays, either within China or, for many, overseas.

For sure, the state is not entirely absent from their lives, but as with Frank and Jessica, it is peripheral most of the time. It is and will remain the supplier of utilities and infrastructure and the ultimate source of law and order.

AT A CROSSROADS

This is exciting but also unnerving. Exciting because it is creating possibilities on a scale never known before. Unnerving because no country has ever experienced anything quite like this before—and no one knows what the outcome will be.

Even the highest-level government officials cannot be sure of the near future. Indeed, official China stands at a crossroads. Can it continue with the hybrid model of government control and economic liberalization that has brought it so much success? Or must it reform further?

The key person responsible for answering this question is Xi Jinping, who emerged as China's paramount leader in November 2012 when he became the general secretary of the Communist Party. In March 2013, he was appointed president. Xi's partner, Premier Li Keqiang, is no lightweight. In particular, when it comes to economic policy, he is widely regarded as an important figure in pushing through market-oriented reforms and other forms of openness that will expose China to more outside competition. But there should be no doubt that Xi is the dominant figure of the two.

Xi unveiled his vision for the next decade—the maximum

term he is permitted in office—in November 2013 at the Third Plenum of the 18th Party Congress. The 60-point document that emerged from the meeting itemized the economic and social agenda Xi wishes to pursue while he serves as party leader and national president. Among its declarations, it indicated that state companies would no longer enjoy many of the privileges, such as protected markets, which until then had allowed many to prosper despite underperforming. Further confirmation came with the announcement at the Third Plenum that the role of the market in economic decision-making would be "decisive."

Xi seems to have concluded that, while political control must remain solely in the hands of the Communist Party, only greater economic freedom can ensure China's continued economic development. In order to maintain growth, the private sector will have to be given a far freer hand. Entrepreneurs know this and sense that opportunities could arise. But they also know that the state resents anyone who tries to usurp its power. Moreover, although the plenum's resolution clearly stated that the market would henceforth play the decisive role in determining how resources are allocated, it also stressed that public ownership would remain the dominant force in the economy. The contradiction between these two elements points to future conflicts.

This report is one of many indicators that the country will continue to open and liberalize its markets. To keep growth coming, more and more sectors will allow ever greater non-state participation, opening the way for further expansion of the private sector and Chinese entrepreneurialism.

There is also the question of whether Xi's efforts to make the country's big state-owned enterprises more efficient will actually work. These organizations remain hugely powerful vested interests.

However, China's development is not just about removing state power—it also calls for enhancing it. Here, scale can create problems as well as bring advantages. China's very size makes it hard for the central government's writ to reach every corner. Many localities can get away with allowing factories to pollute or companies to pirate goods even as officials try to clean up the country and strengthen its intellectual-property regime in ways that will benefit domestic technology companies.

There will be particularly large growth in the service sector. Today, these industries, including telecommunications and finance, are dominated by the state. While private companies' share of industrial investment has risen from around 40 percent a decade ago to two-thirds now, in service industries it has risen far more slowly, from just over 30 percent to around 36 percent.

The single most important reason for this is simply that many key service industries remain largely off-limits to private companies. Despite the recent inroads made by private companies such as Youku Tudou, Noah Wealth Management, Alibaba's Yu'e Bao, Tencent's WeChat, and Geely Auto, their respective sectors are all overwhelmingly dominated by state-owned firms with revenues and resources that dwarf those of even their biggest private rivals. Tencent's total revenues in 2013 were just under $10 billion; those of China Mobile, the world's biggest mobile operator, were more than 10 times greater at just over $100 billion.

For the government to keep economic growth expanding strongly, its best policy would be to liberalize market entry to service sectors. Change is coming in some areas. In health care, as I noted in Chapter 5, the number of private hospitals is rising sharply. But deregulation of finance is happening at a far slower pace, in telecom services it is happening barely at all, and in the media the trend might be reversing: in late 2014, officials introduced rules restricting the amount of overseas programming that online video services could carry.

A PARTNERSHIP BETWEEN ENTREPRENEURS AND THE STATE?

The government must address the future of its decades-long partnership with state-owned enterprises. Though that partnership is weakening, it has far from disappeared. The government clearly still has major hopes for its biggest and best state-owned industries. It would love, for example, for the Commercial Aircraft Corporation of China (COMAC) and its other publicly owned aerospace firms to be able to take on Boeing and Airbus. And such businesses should not be written off; after decades of investment, COMAC's C919 narrow-bodied, single-aisle passenger aircraft, designed to compete with the Boeing 737 and Airbus A320, should go into commercial production by the end of 2015.

But what is changing is the government's view of what it can expect from entrepreneurs, and this is having an effect on its relationship with state-owned enterprises.

President Xi Jinping appears to recognize that China's development will be best served by government ecouragment of the private sector. Support for this part of the economy will help the country tackle such challenges as navigating its way through the middle-income trap—the tricky stage of development that would raise per capita GDP from $10,000 to the high-income level of around $20,000—and transforming its disciplined, labor-intensive manufacturing industries that make low-priced export goods into ones with the flexibility, creativity, and skilled staff that are the prerequisites for building a developed nation.

Relying on exports alone to overcome the middle-income trap is tricky. Instead, companies need to ride increasing sophistication in their home markets up the value chain, producing more complex goods as people in China become richer.

In this, the country's continued drive toward urbanization works in its favor. The November 2013 plenum, among its various radical measures, called for another one-fifth of China's population to leave the countryside, a measure it is enabling by relaxing residency controls in smaller and medium-sized cities.

The government's investment in the education system will also pay off. China is not simply producing more graduates than it needs. It is generating a business environment in which young people like Jessica Wong and Frank Yao can start businesses with a reasonable hope of being successful. Rather than producing a generation of people with degrees working in fast-food restaurants, China will have a soundly educated workforce that is hungry for work. And when they see the opportunities around them, they will be willing to venture out and create work through start-ups and business enterprises of their own, especially in the service sector.

Chinese tradition should also help, especially its long history of encouraging smaller businesses, visible in Taiwan's hugely successful electronics industry and Hong Kong's light-industrial firms, almost all of which now operate mostly in China. Think also of the countless Chinese who have left the country to work as traders across Southeast Asia and beyond.

To call the relationship between the Chinese government and

entrepreneurs a partnership is too strong, but the government is clearly working toward making life substantially easier for private companies. Its abolition of registered capital requirements in early 2014, combined with the removal of much other red tape, has already led to new private companies being set up at the fastest rate since 2005.

In 2013, Premier Li Keqiang pledged that within one year the number of investment projects requiring examination and approval by the State Council would be cut by one-third; one year later the actual figure was 40 percent. Reforms announced at the Communist Party's Third Plenum in November 2013 should also eventually result in more credit being made available to smaller private firms. As of late 2014, these had had little visible impact, though moves such as the establishment of five non-state banks targeted specifically at lending to private sectors— among them the one half-owned by Alibaba—suggest that progress, while slow, is taking place.

As private companies have better returns than state-owned ones, this will stimulate further growth and private consumption. Private companies are also far better placed both to innovate and to take advantage of the opportunities created by innovation. As a result, private companies will see greater increases in productivity than companies under greater state control. Privately held, entrepreneurial companies will thus increase their share of the economy.

Indeed, one of the likely results of allowing market forces to determine the allocation of resources and capital is that many of the hundreds of thousands of state-owned companies owned by local governments will either be closed or sold to better-performing private companies. Over the next decade, China will see further shrinkage in the number of state-owned companies, possibly matching the halving in total number seen in the last decade.

ENTREPRENEURS AND ECONOMIC GROWTH

At age 54, Zhang Yue, the CEO and chairman of Broad Group, is one of China's veteran entrepreneurs. After graduating from a provincial university in the mid 1980s, and working for a period as a librarian and a teacher, he went into business in 1988, starting a boiler-making business with $3,000 borrowed from friends and relatives. Over the next two decades, he expanded his boiler business into one of the world's leading manufacturers of non-electric air conditioners—a technology widely used in factories and other large buildings. As his company grew, he bought luxury cars, private jets, and helicopters, and built copies of Egypt's Great Pyramid and France's Versailles palace at Broad Town, his company's headquarters and principal manufacturing site on the edge of Changsha, the capital of central China's Hunan Province.

In the late 1990s, Zhang visited air-conditioning installations all over the world on the hunt for innovations. These trips led him to see that advances in energy efficiency from better air-conditioning were quite limited. To make big improvements, it would be necessary to improve buildings themselves. He was inspired by communities in Germany and Japan that were making strides in creating energy-efficient buildings and sustainability. Zhang returned from these travels and set his engineers to work on designing those types of buildings.

A further epiphany came in 2008 with the devastating earthquake that hit west China's Sichuan Province, killing around 88,000 people. Cities had to be rebuilt, and Zhang figured out that by using state-of-the-art insulation, light-emitting-diode lights, elevators that generated power, and his own company's cooling and air-filtration technologies, he could create buildings five times more energy-efficient than the tower blocks China is now building.

The following year, Zhang launched Broad Sustainable Building, tasking it with developing prefabricated building units that could be combined into low-energy, environmentally friendly buildings in astonishingly short times. It has built a half dozen test buildings to date, most famously a 30-story hotel whose 15-day construction period was captured on a time-lapse video widely shared around the Internet.

Broad's prefabricated building units, if they come into widespread use, would dramatically reduce energy usage, material wastage, and pollution. Its use of innovative insulation materials, LED lighting, power-generating lifts, and heat-recovery equipment cut energy needs by up to 80 percent for air-conditioning and heating, while the steel, which makes up the main part of the structure, rather than the concrete used in most buildings, can be recycled when the building comes to the end of its life

In 2012, Broad announced plans to build Sky City, designed to be the world's tallest building, also in Changsha. Its blueprints suggest that the building, reaching some 202 stories and 838 meters (2,750 feet) into the sky, could house up to 17,400 people in its 5,000 apartments. Moving them up and down would be 104 elevators. The building was originally scheduled to be completed in just 10 months, but officials halted work on the project shortly after site preparation started in 2013, citing a range of safety concerns related to its novel engineering techniques and the fact that Broad has never built anything taller than its 30-story hotel.

While it's too early to tell whether Sky City will ever be completed, Zhang Yue's approach to the project epitomizes the way in which China's most ambitious business leaders go about their work. Given the continuing growth and ever greater complexity of the China market and its hyperintensive competition, especially in its open sectors, he has to be on the search for new things to do and new ways of doing them that will allow them to leapfrog over others both domestically and internationally.

Zhang Yue is not alone in his search for disruptive innovations. Victor Koo's Youku Tudou also offers a glimpse of just how different China will be in the not-so-distant future. His company offers people freedom to watch videos of their choice, anytime and from anywhere. Along with all the various forms of social media and messaging apps available to people in China, plus the e-commerce option, Yukou Tudou and China's other online video services are already watched more on mobile devices than on computers, a trend that will become more pronounced as hundreds of millions of new smartphones and tablets are sold in China in the next few years.

No longer can the Communist Party force people only to watch what it deems appropriate. Instead, people can choose to go off and watch something completely different. The range of media available is as broad as that found on YouTube, extending from hit domestic television dramas to Western imports such as *Desperate Housewives* and *The X Factor*. It is hard to envisage how radical this would have been even just a few years ago. Official control over what is shown is indirect: Web sites showing streaming videos need a license to operate from the State Administration of Press, Publication, Radio, Film, and Television, and from March 2015 they will have to register all overseas film and TV content they intend to show. Occasionally officials order companies to remove specific programs from their sites, and in 2014 they announced plans to limit foreign programs to 30 percent of all programs offered, but largely the sites are left to police themselves.

Of course, one of the reasons why official China tolerates so much freedom is because it believes it continues to exercise final control. That belief also stems from a confidence that it will not face mass unrest. For sure, there are people who are unhappy in China. As is frequently reported overseas, the number of protests, peaceful and otherwise, number in the tens of thousands each year. But to interpret this as meaning that China stands at the brink of chaos is to totally misread the state of the nation. While overseas, particularly in the West, China is routinely described as a country lacking in basic freedoms and rights, in China the prevailing view is that the country is on the rise, living standards are improving, and as a result personal freedom is also far greater than ever before. Surveys of China by the Pew Research Center have repeatedly found that the country's people are among the happiest in the world both with their current economic situation and with their prospects for the future. The real threat to China's future is not collapse, but that its rulers will fail to manage their country's development.

Or, as I prefer to put it, the political transition that China will need to make is harder than the economic shift from middle-income to high-income status. This transition is not the oversimplistic move toward a representative democracy that many people outside China view as crucial, but rather the creation of institutions able to cope with the stresses and strains of running a country that will only become more complex over time.

China does have an alternative political tradition of a government bureaucracy supporting an emperor, who is expected to rule in the interests of all his people. That bureaucracy was chosen by merit, through examinations. Certainly the Communist Party likes to appeal to this "centralized" model of rule, even if before the 20th century, power was, for practical reasons of geography, very decentralized. While much effort has been made to strengthen meritocratic methods of advancement, both in companies and officialdom, in the longer run China will almost certainly benefit from opening up to greater competition for political and social ideas.

If anything, however, the problem of such a centralized way of running a country, especially one the size of China, is that the government has to be even more aware of public opinion than in a democracy; and figuring out how to balance the conflicting demands made by different interest groups is even harder, especially in a complicated society with multiple interests that compete for attention and support.

THE BIGGEST CHALLENGES

While the country's scale gives it many advantages, scale alone is not enough. Smart policy-making will also be necessary if the country is to handle the inevitable friction that arises from competing economic and social interests.

Indeed, as I see it, the two biggest challenges facing China are how to manage its institutional development and how to manage the reaction from the rest of the world.

For its institutional development, neither technology nor, in the long term, authoritarian rule will be able to provide the answers. Instead, China needs to develop mechanisms that can adjudicate between legitimate competing interests, such as the daily clashes of interests between companies and officials.

China is producing a generation of experimenters—people who are willing to test things out and see what happens. These people know that the rewards, though unpredictable, can be enormous. They are also by definition risk takers—and have big egos.

Jack Ma has led the way in throwing down the gauntlet to the country's state-dominated banking system with his financial services ambitions. He is also expanding into logistics and delivery networks and smart TV. Several of China's Internet video companies are investing or expanding into content production, threatening the long dominance of China's big state-controlled broadcasters.

Although most entrepreneurs explicitly avoid involvement in politics, they also want to make a difference. The most successful—that is to say, those running the biggest companies—will find it all but impossible not to have complicated and tricky negotiations with officials.

One reason is that many corporate leaders, especially older ones, want not just to increase their own wealth but also to improve conditions in China. Broad's Zhang Yue, for example, wants to use his company's prefabricated building units as a way to reduce energy usage, material wastage, pollution, and congestion, hence his Sky City project.

A second threat is China's relationship with the rest of the world. For years, outsiders have claimed that China will not be able to resist openness; as its economy grows, so must its responsiveness to outside forces. That has proven an illusory goal. But if it happens, it is the entrepreneurs of China who will lead the way. A future in which China opens itself to greater freedom of speech and assembly begins with a greater emphasis on global reciprocity to entrepreneurial media. If companies such as Alibaba and Tencent want to go overseas, will China have to open its Internet to Facebook and Twitter?

My guess is yes, though not immediately. In April 2014, Huawei's chief strategy officer, William Xu, predicted that by 2015 the world would have 8 billion smartphone users and 100 billion terminals connected to the Internet. This is a world that will be even more interconnected than it is now—and its entrepreneurs will want it that way.

To avoid any serious backlash, greater policy cooperation will be needed between China and the United States, and possibly, though to a lesser extent, Europe. For China, the big question will be whether to open its investment doors further. Currently, China and the United States are in the early stages of negotiating a bilateral investment treaty that could have as great an impact on investment as China's World Trade Organization entry.

Making this transition will be a challenge. China has long resisted attempts by outside companies or countries to control fully the way they operate within its markets. For example, the Chinese government still wants to retain its "negative" investment list, a list of sectors and industries from which it bars or strictly restricts overseas investment such as finance, Internet, and telecom services. Could this change in the foreseeable future? Certainly, through the China Entrepreneurs Forum and other channels of contact with the government, entrepreneurs will be an important force pushing for greater liberalization.

While inevitably there will be resistance to lowering barriers, entrepreneurs will point out that the greater benefits accruing to them from outbound investment, such as access to overseas markets, technology, and know-how, more than outweigh the losses to Chinese business that might occur if more sectors are opened up to foreign investment in China.

Other kinds of resistance to openness will also emerge. As China moves from being a net importer of capital to being a net exporter, as more of its companies acquire ever greater numbers of businesses around the world, political friction is likely to occur. If the United States, for example, were to start instigating more national security reviews of overseas investment in areas it deems sensitive, then it is easy to envisage China responding by tightening its investment regime rather than loosening it.

As Xi's program makes clear, the Communist Party will retain its role as the leading force running China. Whatever the degree of economic liberalization, it will not surrender its ultimate control over the country's macroeconomic levers.

For example, China will liberalize its financial industry, but on its terms, not those of Western investment banks. And it will keep a leading role for its giant state-owned banks (though I believe that the finance sector will be opened up, at least in part, as a result of entrepreneurial companies moving in).

The government will also remain a hugely important enabler in the way it supports the build-out of infrastructure and encourages meta-projects that will shape entire cities and even regions— such as the rise of Shenzhen across the border from Hong Kong in the 1980s, the emergence of Pudong New Area as Shanghai's financial and industrial heart in the 1990s, and the Go West campaign of the 2000s, which paved the way for the cities of Chengdu and Chongqing to emerge as major centers for investment despite their remote inland locations.

MANAGING THE RISKS

There will be many challenges and uncertainties ahead, especially for individual companies. As Haier's Zhang Ruimin says, "We are taking risks. We may have breakthroughs and become one of the largest new-type companies in the world, or we may fail. I think we can't be called a successful company—but we are reforming and exploring."

Chinese private firms have all the flexibility and entrepreneurial hunger required to compete in consumer and other markets. But they are also focused on growth rather than quality. "China's entrepreneurs are different from those of other countries," says Antony Leung, the CEO of Nan Fung, a Hong Kong–based property and finance group, and the former chairman of Blackstone Group's Asia operations. "They recognize that they operate in a murky environment where rules have not been established, and that they have a responsibility to establish rules as they go along." This lack of rules forces them to be creative—not just always looking to build the next factory, store, or hotel, but to jump into new areas. As a result, internal corporate infrastructure can be very fragile.

A big test for many of them will be an economic slowdown.

China's entrepreneurs have focused almost solely on expansion, says Ricky Lau, a partner at private-equity firm TPG Capital in Hong Kong. "It's all been about building the next store, the next hotel, or the next airport," he says. "The real test will come when it's not about the next store, but how to get existing stores to make more." The government's growth strategy has protected companies from such economic cycles, but without a slowdown, companies can't find out how resilient and robust they are, and this could leave many of them lacking the strength needed to weather a genuine economic crisis.

PROTEAN BODIES

China's ever-changing business environment makes picking long-term winners even more difficult in China than in other countries. Alibaba, Tencent, and Baidu all seem strongly ensconced at the top of China's Internet market, though even their positions are not secure. Having carved out separate empires through the 2010s, the rise of mobile is bringing them into direct competition for the first time, with Tencent in particular clearly eyeing Alibaba's e-commerce crown.

What will help each survive is the great feature they share with almost all of China's entrepreneurial firms: their extraordinary ability to change and adapt. From Zhang Yue's Broad Group to Jessica Wong and Frank Yao's Panda W, these businesses have shown themselves above all to be organizations that can adjust—to the economy, as we have seen repeatedly throughout this book, but also to the ways of those who own and run them.

Lei Jun's Xiaomi has created a business that shapes itself through social media. Alibaba has grown by shaping its next moves according to its own capabilities and the opportunities presented to it. Zhang Ruimin, having taken Haier through three major transitions, is now trying to remake it as a company capable of handling the challenges of the Internet.

Of course, there are many other companies that aren't nearly as fluid. But one of the features of the Chinese business environment is that it demands that organizations be flexible and ready to change—that they be protean. And it's not just companies. Other organizations are similarly fluid; even the government is changing. The Communist Party has reorganized itself since its near-death experience in June 1989 as a body that is capable of change and evolution. Studying how organizations, especially ruling parties, have survived a long time has been a major preoccupation of the Chinese leadership in recent years.

THE NATURE OF SUCCESS

China's entrepreneurs will be the key force driving the country forward through the coming decades, giving China the capabilities it needs. But their spirit of entrepreneurialism runs through more than just its businesses. It manifests itself in the government, and, indeed, in the desires of ordinary people, all of whom share the dream of seeing their country reclaim its place as one of the world's great sources of scientific ideas, technological advances, and ways of doing things.

In this, I am not offering a prediction of the future. Rather, I propose the hypothesis that China has the potential to emerge as a key force determining the direction the world will take through the 21st century, and the reason for this is the role that has been assumed in the country's development by its entrepreneurs. In the process, they will remake the world—not because they want to remake the world, but because such is the interconnectedness of our world, and such is China's scale, that they cannot realize their potential without remaking China, and they cannot remake China without changing the world. In addition to China's and their own resources, they will need resources from the rest of the world—physical resources, such as materials and energy supplies, but also mental resources, including ideas, practices, knowledge, and expertise. China's entrepreneurialism, shaped by the country's history and culture, both short term and long term, is now inevitably going to intermix with global entrepreneurialism.

As this happens, China's entrepreneurs will not be able to ignore the most pressing problems facing the world, above all climate change and the environmental stress generated as more and more people become richer and richer, consuming more of everything. They will have to be actively involved in solving these problems. Because of this, thanks to its entrepreneurs, China will be one of the leading sources of the thinking and practices that will be needed to overcome the great challenges the world will face in the coming decades.

We know that the world is interdependent and, barring disaster, will only become more so. The question therefore is how and on what sort of terms should other countries engage China and should China engage other countries? Given China's rate of economic growth, and the fact that it will soon overtake the United States and become the world's biggest economy, the initial reaction in much of the West is to see it as a threat.

Indeed, already it is clear that it is difficult for many in

America and Europe to view with equanimity a world in which a new power with its own agenda is emerging. The current world was shaped by ideas that came out of Europe and America in the 18th, 19th, and 20th centuries. But now, with the emergence of Asia, and especially China, as the center of global economic gravity, we badly need new thinking. With the West looking ever less confident about its position and decreasingly viewed as a credible leadership source in many parts of the world, this creates an opportunity for revolutionary new approaches and practices. Despite all the fears about the rise of a powerful China, the rest of the world needs to think about how to react to this change. What I propose is that other countries need to look at China's reemergence from a broader perspective, as something rather more than an economic story. They need to see that China's entrepreneurs are also driving a renaissance that will have wide-ranging impacts in a host of fields, many of which they too can benefit from.

A NEW TANG DYNASTY?

I believe that as a consequence of the opening driven by China's entrepreneurs, the push to invest in science, research, and development, and the new freedoms that people are enjoying across the country, China has embarked on a renaissance that could rival its greatest era in history—the Tang dynasty of 618 to 907. Over three centuries, China enjoyed a golden age of economic advancement, openness to the world, and a tremendous cultural flowering. This time around, however, China's flowering could extend much further—with the country playing a crucial role in shaping global well-being and even governance.

With its population, its economic clout, and above all the ambition of its entrepreneurial people, China has the potential to be one of the leaders addressing the global problems of international governance, climate change, and related issues such as food, energy, and resource security. But first it must finish the task of bringing its economy into the 21st century. It may already, by some measures, be the world's largest economic power, but it is still far from fully developed. Per capita income is just one-eighth of America's, and impressive as its progress has been, it is not yet anywhere near fulfilling its potential as a transformative, innovative economic engine.

As we have seen, the country's private sector is already its main driver of growth. China will have to continue liberalizing its economy, both internally and in its economic relations with the rest of the world. Consequently, Xi Jinping's most crucial decisions will be those that determine whether this happens or not. In particular, he must achieve reforms in three key areas. First, financial reforms that liberalize interest rates and compel banks to lend to those businesses which can best use the money rather than those with the best connections. Second, the continuing deregulation of restricted industries, allowing private businesses into sectors such as telecom services. And third, strengthening the legal system and making its operation more transparent so entrepreneurs can trust that their companies will be allowed to operate without official harassment and that their ownership rights are secure—in their businesses, in the intellectual property they generate, and in any wealth they make.

With these three reforms in place, China's entrepreneurs will be able to move toward making the long-term investments that China's economy will need if it is to move on to the next stage of development. From being companies with the capabilities to act and react incredibly quickly to China's changing conditions, they will have to become businesses with longer time horizons. They will have to spend more on research and new product development; they will have to commit to building brands, distribution networks, and the other essential elements of sales and marketing; and, most important, they will have to invest in people, developing the skills and teams that can transform today's disruptive businesses into sustainable global enterprises.

As they do, companies and countries around the world will have to adapt to a new reality: that China is no longer a rapidly emerging economy, but a global force. Its entrepreneurs are already throwing down challenges that multinational companies are struggling to meet; the number and range of those challenges can only increase in the coming decades. These new commercial powers will bring with them innovative products, processes, and ways of thinking. Those of their rivals who can shift their ways of thinking to adopt and adapt these new ways will find themselves better equipped to compete both in China's markets and globally. The biggest challenge will be that posed by businesses using the Internet and related digital technologies that bring down barriers between industries such as entertainment, communications, finance, and retailing, opening them both to new entrants and to existing players willing to cross sector boundaries and venture into new areas. We will see multiple industries disrupted in such a manner in the coming years, with China's entrepreneurs at the forefront of this tidal wave of business destruction and creation.

ACKNOWLEDGMENTS

This book is the product of the collective effort and wisdom of a large group of people whose generosity with their time, expertise, support, and ideas shaped and enriched its content.

First and foremost I would like to thank each of the many entrepreneurs who over the last more than 20 years have shared their thoughts and ideas with me on countless occasions. I am particularly indebted to those who agreed to talk formally about their lives and experiences for this book: Chen Dongsheng, Feng Lun, Chen Haibin, Hunter He, Jiang Xisheng, Victor Koo, Ricky Lau, David Li, He Yifan, Huang Nubo, Antony Leung Kam-chung, Mao Zhenhua, Miao Hongbing, Niu Wenwen, Cary Wang, Diane Wang, Wang Jingbo, Victor Wang, Wang Xing, Wang Wei, Jessica Wong, Xu Lianjie, Frank Yao, Yu Gang, Zeng Ming, and Zhang Ruimin.

Zhang Hongtao of the China Entrepreneurs Forum gave invaluable assistance in opening doors, and Clinton Dines and Shane Tedjarati, as ever, gave me the benefit of their sharp insights into the ways in which international businesses are seeing the rise of Chinese entrepreneurial companies.

Jim Levine of Levine Greenberg Rostan once again did a tremendous job linking me with a publisher—Portfolio/Penguin, where Natalie Horbachevsky, Taylor Fleming, and Hannah Kinisky did a first-class job guiding my manuscript through the editorial process and turning it into the finished product you now have in your hands.

My colleagues at Gao Feng Advisory provided continual support during the many months it took to produce this book—I am immensely grateful to them for their tolerance and forbearance at a time when this—my very own entrepreneurial venture—was taking its first steps.

During this book's gestation, Art Kleiner played a crucial role in shaping and sharpening its ideas and content. Simon Cartledge played an invaluable role as consulting editor, helping with everything from establishing this book's structure to polishing its final draft. And Ron Haddock and Jürgen Ringbeck provided invaluable input reviewing the manuscript and pointing out numerous places where it could be improved and strengthened.

I am indebted to Bob Ching, who introduced me to consulting in China over 20 years ago, for his mentorship over the years.

Finally, I am most grateful to Grace, my wife, for her vital support and continuing inspiration.

NOTES

x **legislation defined a private company as a for-profit organization owned by one or more individuals:** For a discussion of the different types of companies in China, see Yingqiu Liu, "Development of Private Entrepreneurship in China: Process, Problems, and Countermeasures," presented at the Global Forum "Entrepreneurship in Asia: 4th U.S.-Japan Dialogue," April 16, 2003, available at http://www.mansfieldfdn.org/backup/programs/program_pdfs/ent_china.pdf (accessed November 17, 2014).

x **Also excluded from this definition are the many other Chinese firms that are in effect private:** These also include shareholding businesses and businesses established in China by the overseas operations of Chinese businesses; both of these categories are negligible in terms of their economic output and numbers of people employed.

xiv **throughout this book, I write the names of these people in the standard Chinese way:** With one exception—venture capitalist Kai-fu Lee, who has long turned his Chinese name on its head, and in English put his given name (Kai-fu) before his family name (Lee).

Introduction: Enterprises of Our Time

3 **The company's revenues:** All figures are for 2013. Whirlpool's revenues that year were $18.8 billion, while its profits were $850 million; Electrolux's were $17 billion and $105 million. Sources: Haier, "About Haier," at http://www.haier.net/en/about_haier/. Whirlpool, http://

files.shareholder.com/downloads/ABEA-5DXEK8/3625408
430x0x730959/153D9242-5CBF-4CCA-B5BD-00867FAF764C/
Whirlpool_2013AR_spreads_.pdf. Electrolux, Annual Report, available at http://group.electrolux.com/en/electrolux-annual-report-2013
-18535/ (all accessed November 12, 2014).

4 **"The workshop didn't even have any windows then"**: From "Haier's Business Model: Innovation in the Internet Era—CEO Zhang
Ruimin's Speech at the 73rd Annual Meeting of the Academy of
Management," August 11, 2013, transcript available at http://test
.haierpeople.cn/english/cms/c-35240.aspx (accessed November 12,
2014).

7 **Assisted by some major international acquisitions:** Haier paid 10
billion yen (about $130 million) for the Sanyo acquisition and approx-
imately $585 million for Fisher & Paykal. See Juro Osawa, "Pana-
sonic to Sell Sanyo Units," *Wall Street Journal*, July 28, 2011,
available at http://online.wsj.com/news/articles/SB10001424053111
904800304576473060080121304, accessed August 26, 2014, and
Rebecca Howard, "Haier Obtains More Than 90% of Fisher &
Paykal Shares," *Wall Street Journal*, November 5, 2012, available at
http://online.wsj.com/news/articles/SB100014240529702043494
04578101793819992784, accessed August 26, 2014.

7 **"This is a time when everything is changing so fast":** Interview
with Zhang Ruimin, Beijing, June 14, 2014.

9 **The Chinese members of the Fortune Global 500:** See http://
fortune.com/global500/ (accessed August 22, 2014).

9 **as various book titles and headlines have suggested:** Martin
Jacques set the tone in 2009 with his *When China Rules The World:
The Rise of the Middle Kingdom and the End of the Western World*
(London: Allen Lane). Among those who have followed him are:
Aaron L. Friedberg, *A Contest for Supremacy: China, America, and
the Struggle for Mastery in Asia* (W. W. Norton: New York, 2011),
Ivan Tselichtchev, *China Versus the West: The Global Power Shift
of the 21st Century* (John Wiley: Singapore, 2012), and Juan
Pablo Cardenal and Heriberto Araujo, *China's Silent Army: The
Pioneers, Traders, Fixers and Workers Who Are Remaking the World
in Beijing's Image* (New York: Crown, 2013), to name just three
of many.

13 **Gome, despite ups and downs, has maintained its position:** See
Bloomberg News, "China's Gome Posts Narrower-Than-Estimated

Loss," March 26, 2013, available at http://www.bloomberg.com/
news/2013-03-25/china-s-gome-posts-annual-loss-amid-online
-business-expansion.html (accessed August 26, 2014).

**14 the private sector accounts for at least three-quarters of China's
economic output:** As I note in the "Author's Note," it is hard to
gauge the size of China's private sector with precision. Even such
authorities on the Chinese economy as Nicholas Lardy, a senior fellow
at the Peterson Institute for International Economics in Washington,
D.C., hedge their bets with estimates as broad as one-third to three-
quarters. See, for example, "Writing China: Nicholas Lardy, 'Markets
Over Mao,'" at http://blogs.wsj.com/chinarealtime/2014/09/02/writ
ing-china-nick-lardy-combats-conventional-wisdom-in-markets
-over-mao/ (accessed September 1, 2014).

14 1.5 million new private companies were set up: See Arthur Kroe-
ber, "Beijing's Misguided Antitrust Game," Gavekal Dragonomics
China Research, August 13, 2014.

14 Profits jumped even more over the same period: This data is for
industrial companies with an annual output value of more than 20
million yuan (about $3.25 million at the current exchange rate). By
excluding the output of the many millions of small industrial
enterprises, the vast majority of which are not state-owned, it
almost certainly underestimates the private sector's share of industrial output.

17 Nicholas Lardy: See Nicholas R. Lardy, *Markets Over Mao: The
Rise of Private Business in China*, Peterson Institute for International Economics, Washington D.C., 2014, page 84.

18 Tencent's WeChat, a social networking tool: WeChat data is
from "Number of Monthly Active WeChat Users from 2nd
Quarter 2010 to 2nd Quarter 2014 (in Millions)," Statista, no date,
available at http://www.statista.com/statistics/255778/number-of-
active-wechat-messenger-accounts/; WhatsApp data is from Amit
Chowdhry, "WhatsApp Hits 500 Million Users," Forbes.com, April
22, 2014, available at http://www.forbes.com/sites/amitchowdhry/
2014/04/22/whatsapp-hits-500-million-users/ (both accessed August
25, 2014).

19 the nearly $250 billion of business: See Li Hui and Major Tian,
"Smackdown! Alibaba vs Amazon vs Ebay," CKGSB Knowledge,
September 19, 2014, at http://knowledge.ckgsb.edu.cn/2014/09/
19/ecommerce/smackdown-alibaba-vs-amazon-vs-ebay/ (accessed

November 5, 2014). In the first quarter of 2014, transaction volume at Taobao and Tmall was up 46 percent over the same period in 2013, see M. Rochan, "Alibaba Picks NYSE over Nasdaq for Mega US IPO," *International Business Times*, June 27, 2014, available at http://www.ibtimes.co.uk/e-commerce-giant-alibaba-picks-nyse-over-nasdaq-mega-us-ipo-1454375 (accessed November 4, 2014).

20 **A 2014 survey of 2,400 drivers:** See Wang Zhuqiong, "Chinese Shoppers Less Loyal to Brands," *China Daily*, July 6, 2012, available at http://usa.chinadaily.com.cn/business/2012-07/06/content _15555959.htm (accessed September 1, 2014), and Kwong Man-ki, "China's Fickle Motorists Confound Carmakers," *South China Morning Post*, September 18, 2014, available at http://www.scmp .com/business/china-business/article/1594871/chinas-fickle -motorists-confound-carmakers (accessed November 3, 2014).

21 **WH Group:** At the time the deal to buy Smithfield was first announced in May 2013, the company's name was Shuanghui International. It renamed itself in January 2014.

22 **Smithfield's CEO, Larry Pope, said he was shocked:** See Associated Press, "Smithfield CEO Surprised by Reaction to China Sale," March 8, 2014, available at http://www.tricities.com/work ittricities/business_news/article_5b2264aa-a72d-11e3-84af-001a4 bcf6878.html (accessed August 26, 2014).

Chapter 1: Anything Is Possible

33 **the world's fourth-biggest technology company by market capitalization:** After Apple, Google, and Microsoft. See "What Is Alibaba?" at http://projects.wsj.com/alibaba/?from=groupmessage &isappinstalled=0 (accessed September 1, 2014).

33 **China's richest person:** Jack Ma's net worth as of October 31, 2014, according to Bloomberg Billionaires at http://www.bloom berg.com/billionaires/ (accessed November 3, 2014).

35 **Across China, Taobao opened bank accounts in branches of every bank in every city:** For a detailed account of how Alibaba launched its Taobao payment system, see Matthew Forney and Laila F. Khawaja's "UnionPay: Breaking the Monopoly," Gavekal Dragonomics in Profile report, April 2014.

35 **Today, Ma's payment system, now known as Alipay:** Alipay handled $519 billion worth of transactions in 2013; see Paul Mozur, "Payment Service Alipay Holds Key to Alibaba's Growth," *Wall Street Journal*, May 7, 2014, available at http://online.wsj.com/articles/SB10001424052702303678404579535840686151748 (accessed November 13, 2014).

37 **"We don't want to be number one in China. We want to be number one in the world":** As reported by Duncan Clark in "The Alibaba IPO Readies for Lift Off," Forbes.com, May 9, 2014, available at http://www.forbes.com/sites/duncanclark/2014/05/09/chocks-away-for-the-alibaba-ipo/ (accessed November 13, 2014).

37 **he persuaded Goldman Sachs to buy 23 percent of the company:** Although Goldman Sachs subsequently sold its stake, Softbank held on to its shares, seeing them rise to be worth more than $58 billion as Alibaba prepared its initial public offering. See Bruce Einhorn, "Masayoshi Son's $58 Billion Payday on Alibaba," *Bloomberg Businessweek*, May 7, 2014, available at http://www.businessweek.com/articles/2014-05-07/masayoshi-sons-58-billion-payday (accessed September 9, 2014).

38 **orders placed through Alibaba Web sites account for around 70 percent of all package deliveries:** See Lulu Yilun Chen, "Alibaba Earnings Surge Boosts Valuation Ahead of IPO," Bloomberg, April 16, 2014, available at http://www.bloomberg.com/news/2014-04-15/alibaba-profit-grows-ahead-of-initial-public-offering.html (accessed September 9, 2014).

39 **Alibaba's total loan book stood at $2 billion:** See "Alibaba's Small Business Lending Moves Ahead," *Wall Street Journal*, July 5, 2013, available at http://online.wsj.com/news/articles/SB10001424127887324260204578587451309343978 (accessed August 28, 2014).

39 **What made Yu'e Bao attractive:** China's central bank, the People's Bank of China, restricts bank-demand deposits to paying annual interest of less than 1 percent, and time deposits to a maximum of just over 3 percent. Yu'e Bao, which can invest in higher-interest-earning money-market funds, has offered returns of up to 6 percent.

39 **Yu'e Bao's arrival, followed shortly after by similar products from China's two other Internet giants, Baidu and Tencent:** See Gabriel Wildau, "China Banks Strike Back Against Threat from Internet Finance," Reuters, February 23, 2014, available at http://

uk.reuters.com/article/2014/02/23/uk-china-banks-online-idUK
BREA1M12I20140223 (accessed February 25, 2014).

40 **"If you plan, you lose. If you don't plan, you win"**: See Duncan
Clark, "The Alibaba IPO Readies for Lift Off," Forbes.com,
May 9, 2014, available at http://www.forbes.com/sites/duncanclark/
2014/05/09/chocks-away-for-the-alibaba-ipo/ (accessed July 30,
2014).

41 **Zeng Ming, Alibaba's chief strategy officer, puts it this way:**
Interview with Zeng Ming, Hangzhou, February 26, 2014.

46 **"I decided to move outside of the system"**: Interview with Feng
Lun, Beijing, December 5, 2013.

49 **"One question is in the mind of every fledgling entrepreneur"**:
See Edward Tse, "China's Five Surprises," *strategy+business*, Winter
2005.

52 **another of China's top 10 richest figures:** Zong Qinghou's net worth
was $11.5 billion as of July 30, 2014, according to the Bloomberg
Billionaires list; see www.bloomberg.com/billionaires/.

53 **But he says he has no regrets:** Interview with Wang Xing, Beijing,
April 12, 2014. Transaction data, see Bloomberg News, "Alibaba-
Backed Buying Site Meituan Considering U.S. IPO," May 12, 2014,
available at http://www.bloomberg.com/news/2014-05-12/alibaba
-backed-buying-site-meituan-eyes-u-s-ipo-as-sales-triple.html (accessed September 4, 2014).

54 **In a series of interviews to Western and Chinese journalists:**
See, for example, Daniel Thomas, "Huawei's Founder Rejects Possibility of Stock Market Listing," *Financial Times*, May 2, 2014,
available at http://www.ft.com/intl/cms/s/0/c67364e2-d1f9-11e3
-8ff4-00144feabdc0.html (accessed February 12, 2015).

55 **"Their love of their country isn't the same as that of the generation before them"**: Interview with Chen Dongsheng, Beijing,
February 21, 2014.

59 **"In the past, the management of Chinese companies was really
simple"**: Interview with Zhang Ruimin, Beijing, June 14, 2014.

60 **"Alibaba was founded with a simple mission"**: See Jack Ma, "Jack
Ma on Taking Back China's Blue Skies," HBR Blog Network,
November 11, 2013, available at http://blogs.hbr.org/2013/11/jack
-ma-on-taking-back-chinas-blue-skies/ (accessed September 1, 2014).

61 **"revolutionized how Chinese people live, learn, work and play"**:
See Jack Ma, "Jack Ma on Taking Back China's Blue Skies," HBR

Blog Network, November 11, 2013, available at http://blogs.hbr
.org/2013/11/jack-ma-on-taking-back-chinas-blue-skies/
(accessed September 1, 2014).

62 **a centuries-long rejection of free-market economics:** For a discussion of this rejection, see David Graeber, *Debt: The First 5,000
Years* (New York: Melville House, 2011), pages 259–260.

Chapter 2: Wide Open

68 **that target was raised to 60 million:** See Josh Horwitz, "Xiaomi
Is Well on Track to Sell 60 Million Smartphones in 2014," TechIn
Asia.com, October 8, 2014, at https://www.techinasia.com/xiaomi
-is-well-on-track-to-sell-60-million-smartphones-in-2014/ (accessed
November 5, 2014).

68 **its valuation up to $40–$50 billion:** See Bloomberg News, "Xiaomi
Said to Seek Funding at About $50 Billion Valuation," November 4,
2014, available at http://www.bloomberg.com/news/2014-11-03/
xiaomi-said-to-seek-funding-at-valuation-of-about-50-billion.html
(accessed November 5, 2014).

69 **Lei told TechHive Web site journalist Michael Kan:** See
Michael Kan, "China's Xiaomi Takes Crowdsourced Phone Development Model Abroad," TechHive, May 8, 2013, at http://www
.techhive.com/article/2038184/chinas-xiaomi-takes-crowdsourced
-phone-development-model-abroad.html (accessed September 9,
2014).

73 **Companies wanting to sell into these markets have released an
extraordinary number of products:** See Edward Tse, *The China
Strategy* (New York: Basic Books, 2010), pages 27–28.

73 **tourism, where the 3 billion trips Chinese now take annually are
expected to double in number by 2020:** For the tourism forecast,
see Lily Kuo, "Five Trends That Could Make China the World's
Largest Consumer Market by 2015," Quartz.com, March 19, 2013,
available at http://qz.com/64610/five-trends-that-could-make-china
-the-worlds-largest-consumer-market-by-2015/, and for the aircraft
forecast, see Tom Mitchell, "Boeing Tips China to Overtake US
as Biggest Aviation Market," *Financial Times*, September 4, 2014,
available at http://www.ft.com/intl/cms/s/0/57d76fa2-3418-11e4
-8832-00144feabdc0.html#axzz3D0EvfkQR (both accessed September 11, 2014).

73 Research by Beijing-based economic research firm Gavekal Dragonomics: See Thomas Gatley, "Accelerating into Affluence," *China Economic Quarterly*, Volume 17, Issue 1, March 2013, pages 46–50.

84 Zhou successfully took on the mobile app market: Qihoo was still the mobile app market leader as of August 2014; see "Qihoo 360 Technology (QIHU) Tops Q2 EPS by 4c; Guides Q3 Revenues Above the Street," StreetInsider.com, August 2014, available at http://www.streetinsider.com/Earnings/Qihoo+360+Technology+%28QIHU%29+Tops+Q2+EPS+by+4c%3B+Guides+Q3+Revenues+Above+the+Street/9778306.html (accessed November 4, 2011).

85 Tencent's CEO, Pony Ma, was comfortably the richer of the two: Bloomberg Billionaires index put Pony Ma's worth at $15.5 billion on September 11, 2014. For his current net worth, see http://www.bloomberg.com/billionaires/.

86 Naspers, which for $32 million acquired a 47 percent stake: Buying this stake proved an extremely lucrative investment. Despite having since being diluted to around 35 percent, Naspers's investment was worth more than $55 billion as of mid 2014.

Chapter 3: Do or Die

93 "Why China Can't Innovate": Regina M. Abrami, William C. Kirby, and F. Warren McFarlan, "Why China Can't Innovate," *Harvard Business Review*, March 2014.

96 e-commerce accounted for 8 percent of China's retail sales: See Newley Purnell, "Southeast Asia E-Commerce Set to Boom," WSJ.D, July 10, 2014, available at http://blogs.wsj.com/digits/2014/07/10/southeast-asia-e-commerce-set-to-boom/ (accessed September 15, 2014).

98 the numbers will fall precipitously as the workforce falls to 650 million: See Ansuya Harjani, "This Is How Fast China's Workforce Is Shrinking," CNBC, January 20, 2014, available at http://www.cnbc.com/id/101349829 (accessed September 2, 2014).

99 Rita Gunther McGrath, a professor at Columbia Business School: See Theodore Kinni, "The Thought Leader Interview: Rita Gunther McGrath," *strategy+business*, Issue 74, Spring 2014.

100 SF Express: See Li Tao-cheng, "SF Express Chain Stores Stir Up China's E-Commerce Market," WantChinaTimes.com, June 3, 2014, available at http://www.wantchinatimes.com/news-subclass-cnt.aspx ?id=20140603000003&cid=1502 (accessed November 4, 2014).

108 **At the higher end, of 200,000 doctorates in science and engineering awarded around the world in 2010:** See "National Science Foundation Science and Engineering Indicators 2014," available at http://www.nsf.gov/statistics/seind14/index.cfm/overview via http://www.universityworldnews.com/article.php?story=20140227152409830 (accessed September 2, 2014).

108 **By 2020, they will form part of a total graduate workforce numbering nearly 200 million:** See David J. Lynch, "Grads Remake China Workforce as High-end Threat to U.S.," Bloomberg, April 17, 2014, at http://www.bloomberg.com/news/2014-04-15/grads -remake-china-workforce-as-high-end-threat-to-u-s-.html (accessed September 2, 2014).

109 **Over the past 20 years China has increased its grain productivity by 2.6 percent annually:** See Xinhua News Agency, "Chinese Innovations to Benefit the World: Bill Gates," April 7, 2014, available at http://www.chinadaily.com.cn/business/2013-04/07/content _16381042.htm (accessed September 2, 2014).

110 **China is now the world's biggest industrial robot market:** See "Industrial Robot Statistics," International Federation of Robotics, 2014, available at http://www.ifr.org/industrial-robots/statistics/ (accessed September 2, 2014).

110 **officials have committed $82 billion over the five years:** See Christina Larson, "China Expected to Be the Top Market for Industrial Robots by 2016," *Bloomberg Businessweek*, November 15, 2013, available at http://www.businessweek.com/articles/2013-11-15/china-expected-to-be-top-market-for-industrial-robots-by-2016 (accessed September 2, 2014).

110 **the world's leading developer of 3D printing technology:** See "China Developing World's Largest 3D Printer, Prints 6m Metal Parts in One Piece," 3ders.org, February 7, 2014, available at http://www.3ders.org/articles/20140207-china-developing -world-largest-3d-printer--prints-6m-metal-parts-in-one-piece .html (accessed September 2, 2014).

113 **Intel Capital announced:** See "Intel Capital Announces Investments of US$28 Million from China Smart Device Innovation Fund," October 21, 2104, at http://www.intelcapital.com/news/ news.html?id=267#/ (accessed November 7, 2014).

120 **By 2014, private companies' share of all outbound investment:** See KPMG, "China Outlook 2015," available at http://www.kpmg .com/CN/en/IssuesAndInsights/ArticlesPublications/Documents/ China-Outlook-2015-201501-v1.pdf (accessed February 13, 2015).

121 **R&D spending by Chinese-owned firms in the United States has also grown fast:** See Daniel H. Rosen and Thilo Hanneman, "New Realities in the US-China Investment Relationship," Rhodium Group/U.S. Chamber of Commerce, April 2014, available at http://rhg.com/wp-content/uploads/2014/04/RHG_New-Realities _29April2014.pdf (accessed October 13, 2014).

126 **Lenovo also acquired 10,000 IBM employees:** see "China: China's Largest Personal Computer Maker, Lenovo Group Ltd, Buys Control of IBM's PC-Making Business," ITN Source, December 8, 2004, available at http://www.itnsource.com/shotlist//rtv/2004/ 12/08/412080012/?s=business (accessed October 13, 2014).

128 **its share of the PC market is only 10 percent:** See Mark Hachman, "Lenovo Widens Lead as PC Market Decline Slows," PCWorld .com, January 10, 2014, available at http://www.pcworld.com/arti cle/2086561/lenovo-widens-lead-as-pc-market-decline-slows .html (accessed October 13, 2014).

130 **Wanxiang Group, China's biggest auto-components maker:** See Liu Chang, "Wanxiang Finds Success in US," *China Daily*, July 28, 2014, available at http://usa.chinadaily.com.cn/2014-07/28/content _17944873.htm (accessed September 22, 2014), and "A123 Systems Announces Non-Binding Memorandum of Understanding with Wanxiang Group Corporation for Strategic Investment," available at http://www.a123systems.com/087cf5d5-5f36-4799-bc66-7d04 f3f4a88d/media-room-2012-press-releases-detail.htm#sthash .ko29eWyv.dpuf (accessed October 13, 2014).

133 **China's best-selling private carmaker:** For a list of China's leading automakers, see Colum Murphy, "Ford's SUVs Propel Its China Gains," *Wall Street Journal*, April 3, 2014, available at http:// online.wsj.com/articles/SB100014240527023035462045794374 44002456878 (accessed November 13, 2014).

137 **Sales of MG cars:** See "2012 New Car Market Tops Two Million Units, a Four-Year High," SMMT.co.uk, January 7, 2013, available at http://www.smmt.co.uk/2013/01/2012-new-car-market-tops-two -million-units-hitting-four-year-high/ (accessed November 7, 2014),

Notes

and "2013 Passenger Vehicle Sales by Brand," ChinaAutoWeb, January 15, 2014, available at http://chinaautoweb.com/2014/01/2013-passenger-vehicle-sales-by-brand/ (accessed November 7, 2014).

138 **carmaker Chery:** Chery was started by a group of Anhui provincial government officials, and—like Haier—is technically a local government-owned business. From the start, however, it has been run like a private business; indeed, for the first four years, before it secured a carmaking license in 2003, its operation was in theory illegal.

139 **Tencent spent $200 million promoting WeChat overseas in both 2013 and 2014:** See Michael Kan, "Tencent to Focus WeChat on Markets Where Competition Isn't Entrenched," PCWorld.com, March 19, 2014, available at http://www.pcworld.com/article/2110260/tencent-to-focus-wechat-on-markets-where-competition-isnt-entrenched.html (accessed September 19, 2014).

139 **Robin Li's Baidu is making a concerted push into new markets:** See Eli Schwartz, "Baidu Expanded into Brazil: Why It's a Great Decision and What It Means for the Future," Search Engine Journal, August 24, 2014, available at http://www.searchenginejournal.com/baidu-expanded-brazil-great-decision-means-future/114011/ (accessed September 19, 2014).

Chapter 5: Changing China

145 **Victor Wang, the chairman of Mtone Wireless:** In China, Victor Wang is better known by his Chinese name, Wang Weijia.

147 **Wang Wei, the founder of China's first mergers and acquisitions firm:** Not to be confused with Wang Wei, the founder of SF Express, China's largest privately owned express delivery business.

147 **economist Lawrence Tian, the founder of China's first futures company:** In China, Lawrence Tian is known as Tian Yuan.

148 **even by 2010, the CEF only had 50 members:** For a full list of the CEF's early members, see the Harvard Business School case study "The China Entrepreneurs Forum" by William C. Kirby, G. A. Donovan, and Tracy Yuen Manty, revised May 14, 2012, pages 10–12.

151 **Current estimates of high-net-worth individuals (HNWIs) in China:** For estimates of the numbers of China's high-net-worth individuals and their wealth, see http://www.bain.com/about/press/press-releases/chinese-high-net-worth-individuals-shift-wealth

-management-focus-from-growing-to-preserving-assets.aspx; http://
export.gov/china/build/groups/public/@eg_cn/documents/web
content/eg_cn_036898.pdf; http://www.prweb.com/releases/2013/
11/prweb11353349.htm (all accessed October 13, 2014).

158 **One study of Chinese television and online video habits in 2013:**
See "China TV and Online Videos Report 2013: Almost Half
Don't Watch TV Any More," China Internet Watch, October 22,
2013, available at http://www.chinainternetwatch.com/4254/china
-tv-online-videos-report-2013/ (accessed October 13, 2014).

158 **China's answer to YouTube:** For YouTube's revenues, see See Jay
Yarrow, "YouTube's Revenue Revealed, and It's Much Worse Than
Expected," July 7, 2014, available at http://www.businessinsider
.com/youtubes-2013-revenue-2014-7 (accessed October 13, 2014).
The forecast doubling in value of China's online video industry is
made by Internet consultant Iresearch; see http://www.bloomberg
.com/news/2014-03-26/tencent-stake-purchase-report-fuels-youku
-most-in-month.html (accessed October 13, 2014).

158 **Its monthly viewership reached 500 million unique visitors in
August 2014:** See Kaylene Hong, "China's Youku Tudou Now Serves
500 Million Users per Month, Half of YouTube's Reach," thenex
tweb.com, August 20, 2014, available at http://thenextweb.com/asia/
2014/08/20/chinas-youku-tudou-now-serves-500-million-users-per
-month-half-of-youtubes-reach/ (accessed September 26, 2014).

159 **Youku resumed its money-losing ways:** For 2013 as a whole,
Youku Tudou lost just under $100 million, sharply down from the
$427 million of 2012. In the first quarter of 2014, its net loss was
$36 million, and in the second quarter it was $27 million. See
PR Newswire, "Youku Tudou Announces First Quarter 2014
Unaudited Financial Results," available at http://www.prnewswire
.com/news-releases/youku-tudou-announces-first-quarter-2014
-unaudi ted-financial-results-260330571.html, and "Youku Tudou
Announces Second Quarter 2014 Unaudited Financial Results,"
available at http://www.prnewswire.com/news-releases/youku-tudou
-announces-second-quarter-2014-unaudited-financial-results
-271911851.html (both accessed November 6, 2014).

159 **By early 2014, consumers were watching around 45 billion minutes a month on the Youku App mobile video application:** See
"iResearch: Youku 3rd Most Popular App in China," Media Research
Asia, March 31, 2014, available at http://www.mediaresearchasia
.com/view.php?type=press&id=3449 (accessed October 13, 2014).

160 **Youku spends around 35 to 40 percent of revenues on content:**
See Eric Jhonsa, "Youku Slumps amid Video Traffic Worries,"
Seekingalpha.com, April 4, 2014, available at http://seekingalpha
.com/news/1661153-youku-slumps-amid-video-traffic-worries
(accessed October 13, 2014).

160 **"Our subscriber base," Koo told *Variety*:** See Patrick Frater, "Youku
Tudou CEO Victor Koo Talks Streaming Company's Cross-Platform
Plans," *Variety*, September 5, 2014, available at http://variety.com/
2014/digital/news/youku-tudou-executive-victor-koo-interview
-1201296375/ (accessed Novembver 13, 2014).

160 **some 2 million "public opinion analysts" :** See "China Employs
Two Million Microblog Monitors State Media Say," BBC.com,
October 4, 2013, available at http://www.bbc.com/news/world-asia
-china-24396957 (accessed October 13, 2014).

162 **seven months later announced that Lei Jun's Xiaomi:** See Paul
Carsten and Gerry Shih, "Xiaomi to Buy Stake in Youku Tudou as
Part of Online Video Push," Reuters, November 12, 2014, available at
http://www.reuters.com/article/2014/11/12/us-youku-tudou-xiaomi
-idUSKCN0IW0KY20141112 (accessed November 17, 2014).

170 **Wang was also detained:** He was subsequently released on bail in
early 2014; at the time of going to press, a time for a trial had yet to
be set.

171 **"My view is that the Chinese government should adopt a more
systematic and comprehensive approach":** See Kiran Moodley,
"China Just Went Through a 'Lost Decade': Entrepreneurs," CNBC,
April 22, 2013, available at http://www.globalpost.com/dispatch/
news/regions/asia-pacific/china/130422/economic-growth
-entre preneurs (accessed October 13, 2014).

Chapter 6: The Right Response

175 **says Xu Lianjie with a chuckle:** Xu is also known, particularly in
Hong Kong, as Hui Lin Chit, the Cantonese transliteration of his
name. As he is usually referred to in China as Xu Lianjie, and that
is the transcription he uses on his business card; I have preferred to
use this romanization of his name.

181 **both U.S. and European investment into China appeared to be
catching its breath:** See "European Firms Are Adapting to a New
Sober Reality in China by Revising Down Expectations and Investment Plans," Roland Berger Strategy Consultants, June 2, 2014,

available at http://www.rolandberger.com/press_releases/514-press
_archive2014_sc_content/European_firms_adapting_to_sober
_reality_in_China.html (accessed July 15, 2013).

192 **There are currently more than 1,300 R&D centers established
by multinationals in China:** See KPMG, "Innovated in China:
New Frontier for Global R&D," August 2013, available at http://
www.kpmg.com/DE/de/Documents/China-360-Issue11-201308
-new-frontier-for-global-R-and-D-2013-KPMG.pdf (accessed July
21, 2014).

193 **Honeywell has invested more than half a billion dollars:** See
http://honeywell.com/About/Pages/global-presence.aspx (accessed
July 9, 2014). For more on Honeywell's China-based R&D and
product development see Edward Tse, *The China Strategy* (New
York: Basic Books, 2010), pages 137–38.

194 **the 34 percent of Tencent bought by South African media group
Naspers:** Naspers originally bought a 46.5 percent stake in Tencent; this was subsequently diluted to 34 percent.

194 **the stakes held in Alibaba by Softbank (32 percent) and Yahoo
(22.6 percent stake):** Singapore's government investment company,
Temasek, and Russian technology fund DST also have smaller
stakes in Alibaba. See Sarah Miskin, "Show Me the Money: Alibaba's Top Shareholders," *Financial Times*, May 7, 2014.

194 **chocolate maker Hershey committed $577 million to buy
Golden Monkey:** See: "Hershey Completes Initial Purchase of
Shanghai Golden Monkey Food Joint Stock Co., Ltd.," Business-
Wire, September 25, 2014, available at http://www.businesswire
.com/news/home/20140925006102/en/Hershey-Completes-Initial
-Purchase-Shanghai-Golden-Monkey#.VH72GcklHEw (accessed
December 3, 2014).

194 **Shanghai-based conglomerate Fosun bought a stake of just
under 10 percent of Club Med:** At the time of writing, Fosun had
raised its stake in Club Med to 18 percent and was locked in a
battle for control of the company with Investindustrial, a private-
equity firm run by Italian investor Andrea Bonomi. If its bid to
acquire Club Med were to succeed, Fosun would end up owning
85 percent of the company. See Adam Thomson and Patti Wald-
meir, "Fosun Restarts Club Med Takeover Battle with Higher
Bid," FT.com, September 12, 2014, available at http://www.ft.com/
intl/cms/s/0/b7eaaa24-3a5f-11e4-bd08-00144feabdc0.html#ax
zz3JHvttDgd (accessed November 17, 2014).

212 **private companies' share of industrial investment:** See Nicholas R. Lardy, *Markets over Mao: The Rise of Private Business in China*, Peterson Institute for International Economics, Washington D.C., 2014, page 133.

217 **a time-lapse video:** This can be seen on Broad's Web site at http://en.broad.com/video.html?3 (accessed November 7, 2014).

219 **Surveys of China by the Pew Research Center:** See Katie Simmons, "China's Government May Be Communist, but Its People Embrace Capitalism," Pew Research Center, October 14, 2014, available at http://www.pewresearch.org/fact-tank/2014/10/10/chinas-government-may-be-communist-but-its-people-embrace-capitalism/ (accessed November 14, 2014).

224 **Antony Leung, the CEO of Nan Fung:** Interview, November 13, 2013.

225 **Ricky Lau, a partner at private-equity firm TPG Capital:** Interview, December 9, 2013.

INDEX

Page numbers in *italics* refer to figures and tables.